Dr. George Shaw.

LANCING COLLEGE

*Homing Cottage, North Bersted.*

# Around Historic Sussex

Drawings by Gerald Lip

EAGLE PUBLISHING COMPANY

The superbly illustrated pen and ink drawings by Gerald Lip contained in this informative and easily read book have been selected from a series which has appeared in the Evening Argus every Friday for the past 13 years. The series is currently being written by James Forlong a journalist with the newspaper.

Gerald Lip was educated at Harrow School of Art and exhibited at the Royal Academy at a very early age, he is now cartoon editor of a well known national newspaper group. He was also art instructor at Army College North, Welbeck Abbey during his stint in the army. Much of his work has appeared in national newspapers and magazines throughout the years. Gerald Lip lives with his wife and young daughter in Hove.

*Highbridge Mill, Cuckfield.*

**First published in 1982 by**
**EAGLE PUBLISHING COMPANY**
**63b Lansdowne Place, Hove, Sussex.**

**Gerald Lip 1982.**

**ISBN 0 905782 05 4.**

Printed and bound in Great Britain at The Pitman Press, Bath

# FOREWORD

by Andrew Bowden, M.B.E., M.P.

*Member of Parliament for Kemp Town, Brighton.*

*Ye Olde Pump House, Hastings.*

HOUSE OF COMMONS
LONDON SWIA OAA

I have admired the work of Gerald Lip for many years. I am delighted to recommend this little gem of a book, so beautifully illustrated with the drawings of Gerald Lip and with articles full of historical and fascinating detail, altogether a mine of information. It is a pleasure to read and a feast for the eye. With this enchanting book as your travelling companion you will never be lost for ideas and places to visit in Sussex.

# Contents
# and
# Illustrations

*Garden loggia at Slaugham Place.*

The West Pier, Brighton ........................ Front cover
Landgate, Rye ............................. Back cover
North Bersted, Homing Cottage ........................... 1
Cuckfield, Highbridge Mill .............................. 2
Hastings, Ye Olde Pump House ......................... 3
Foreward, Andrew Bowden, MBE, MP ................... 3
Slaugham Place ....................................... 4
Bramber, Bramber Castle Hotel ......................... 5
Billingshurst, Sayers Farm ............................. 6
Aldingbourne Mill ..................................... 7
Alfriston, Moonrakers ................................. 8
Alfriston, St. Andrew's ................................ 9
Amberley, Stream Cottage............................. 10

Amberley, Castle ................................... 11
Angmering, Pigeon House ........................... 12
Appledram, Rymans ................................ 13
Ardingly, Wakehurst Place .......................... 14
Arundel Castle ..................................... 15
Arundel Cathedral .................................. 16
Arundel Emporium .................................. 17
Arundel, 10 Maltravers Street........................ 18
Ashurst, Blocques .................................. 19
Balcombe, White House.............................. 20
Battle Hospital ..................................... 21
Billingshurst, Jennie Wren Restaurant................. 22
Birling Gap, Seven Sisters ........................... 23
Bodiam Castle ..................................... 24
Bolney, Wykehurst Park.............................. 25
Bramber, Lavender Cottage........................... 26
Brighton, The Royal Pavilion ......................... 27
Brighton, Volk's Railway ............................. 28
Brighton, The Old Ship Hotel ......................... 29
Brighton, Theatre Royal .............................. 30
Brighton, Regency Square ............................ 31
Brighton, Royal Crescent ............................ 32
Brighton, Grand Hotel ............................... 33
Brighton, Holy Trinity Church ........................ 34
Brighton/Hove, Peace Statue.......................... 35
Burgess Hill, Hammonds Place........................ 36
Burpham Church .................................... 37
Bury House ........................................ 38
Chailey, Five Bells .................................. 39
Chichester Cathedral................................. 40
Chichester, Grey Friars Chancel ...................... 41
Chiddingly, Cobwebs Cottage ........................ 42
Climping, Bailiffscourt .............................. 43
Cooden Beach, Barnhorne Manor ..................... 44
Cooksbridge, Rainbow Inn............................ 45
Cowbeech, Cowbeech House .......................... 46
Cowfold, St. Peter's Cottage ......................... 47
Cowfold, Clock House ............................... 48
Cross Bush, Convent of Poor Clares ................... 49
Crowborough, Windlesham Manor ..................... 50
Cuckfield, Tower House .............................. 51
Ditchling, Anne of Cleves' House ..................... 52
Ditchling, Wild Goose Cottage........................ 53

*Sayers Farm, Billingshurst.*

Ditchling, The Old Meeting House . . . . . . . . . . . . . . . . . . . . . 54
Eastbourne Pier . . . . . . . . . . . . . . . . . . . . . . . . . . . . . . . . . . . . 55
Eastbourne, Belle Tout. . . . . . . . . . . . . . . . . . . . . . . . . . . . . . . 56
Eastbourne Town Hall . . . . . . . . . . . . . . . . . . . . . . . . . . . . . . . 57
Eastbourne, The Burlington Hotel . . . . . . . . . . . . . . . . . . . . . 58
East Grinstead, Old Stone House . . . . . . . . . . . . . . . . . . . . . . 59
Felpham, William Blake's Cottage. . . . . . . . . . . . . . . . . . . . . . 60
Findon Place Manor . . . . . . . . . . . . . . . . . . . . . . . . . . . . . . . . . 61
Firle Place, Nr Lewes . . . . . . . . . . . . . . . . . . . . . . . . . . . . . . . . 62
Fittleworth, Coates Castle . . . . . . . . . . . . . . . . . . . . . . . . . . . . 63
Glynde Church. . . . . . . . . . . . . . . . . . . . . . . . . . . . . . . . . . . . . . 64
Goodwood House . . . . . . . . . . . . . . . . . . . . . . . . . . . . . . . . . . . 65
Graffham . . . . . . . . . . . . . . . . . . . . . . . . . . . . . . . . . . . . . . . . . . 66
Greatham, Quell Farm . . . . . . . . . . . . . . . . . . . . . . . . . . . . . . . 67
Groombridge, Penns in the Rocks . . . . . . . . . . . . . . . . . . . . . . 68
Guestling, Brooham School . . . . . . . . . . . . . . . . . . . . . . . . . . . 69
Hailsham, Windmill Hill Place . . . . . . . . . . . . . . . . . . . . . . . . 70
Handcross, High Beeches. . . . . . . . . . . . . . . . . . . . . . . . . . . . . 71
Hartfield, Cotchford Farm . . . . . . . . . . . . . . . . . . . . . . . . . . . . 72
Henfield, Mockbridge House . . . . . . . . . . . . . . . . . . . . . . . . . . 73
Henfield, St. Giles Church. . . . . . . . . . . . . . . . . . . . . . . . . . . . 74

Henfield, Woods Mill . . . . . . . . . . . . . . . . . . . . . . . . . . . . . . . . 75
Horsham, Christ's Hospital . . . . . . . . . . . . . . . . . . . . . . . . . . . 76
Horsham, Knepp Castle . . . . . . . . . . . . . . . . . . . . . . . . . . . . . . 77
Horsted Keynes, Ludwell Grange . . . . . . . . . . . . . . . . . . . . . . 78
Horsted Keynes, The Old House . . . . . . . . . . . . . . . . . . . . . . . 79
Houghton, Old Farm. . . . . . . . . . . . . . . . . . . . . . . . . . . . . . . . . 80
Houghton, Houghton House . . . . . . . . . . . . . . . . . . . . . . . . . . 81
Hove, Brunswick Square . . . . . . . . . . . . . . . . . . . . . . . . . . . . . 82
Hove, Museum of Art. . . . . . . . . . . . . . . . . . . . . . . . . . . . . . . . 83
Hove, Lansworth House. . . . . . . . . . . . . . . . . . . . . . . . . . . . . . 84
Hurstpierpoint, Danny House . . . . . . . . . . . . . . . . . . . . . . . . . 85
Hurstpierpoint, Pakyns Manor . . . . . . . . . . . . . . . . . . . . . . . . 86
Hurstpierpoint, Pigwidgeon Cottage. . . . . . . . . . . . . . . . . . . . 87
Hurstpierpoint, The Tower . . . . . . . . . . . . . . . . . . . . . . . . . . . 88
Hurstpierpoint, Randolphs Farm . . . . . . . . . . . . . . . . . . . . . . 89
Keymer, The Mill . . . . . . . . . . . . . . . . . . . . . . . . . . . . . . . . . . . 90
Keymer, St. Cosmas and St. Damian Church . . . . . . . . . . . . 91
Lancing, The Old Posting House . . . . . . . . . . . . . . . . . . . . . . 92
Lewes, Keere Street . . . . . . . . . . . . . . . . . . . . . . . . . . . . . . . . . 93
Lewes, Southover Grange . . . . . . . . . . . . . . . . . . . . . . . . . . . . 94
Lewes, St. Michael's Church. . . . . . . . . . . . . . . . . . . . . . . . . . 95
Lindfield, Paxhill Park . . . . . . . . . . . . . . . . . . . . . . . . . . . . . . . 96
Lindfield, East Mascalls. . . . . . . . . . . . . . . . . . . . . . . . . . . . . . 97
Lindfield, The Thatched Cottage . . . . . . . . . . . . . . . . . . . . . . 98
Lindfield, Humphrey's Bakery . . . . . . . . . . . . . . . . . . . . . . . . 99
Lindfield, Cockhaise Mill Farm . . . . . . . . . . . . . . . . . . . . . . 100
Midhurst, Spread Eagle Hotel . . . . . . . . . . . . . . . . . . . . . . . 101
Midhurst, The Wheatsheaf . . . . . . . . . . . . . . . . . . . . . . . . . . 102
Newhaven, The Bridge Inn . . . . . . . . . . . . . . . . . . . . . . . . . . 103
Newick, Founthill Farm. . . . . . . . . . . . . . . . . . . . . . . . . . . . . 104
Northiam, Great Dixter . . . . . . . . . . . . . . . . . . . . . . . . . . . . . 105
Patcham, All Saints Church . . . . . . . . . . . . . . . . . . . . . . . . . 106
Petworth House . . . . . . . . . . . . . . . . . . . . . . . . . . . . . . . . . . . 107
Petworth, London & County Bank. . . . . . . . . . . . . . . . . . . . 108
Petworth, Church of St. Mary. . . . . . . . . . . . . . . . . . . . . . . . 109
Pevensey Museum. . . . . . . . . . . . . . . . . . . . . . . . . . . . . . . . . 110
Poynings, Dyke Farm House . . . . . . . . . . . . . . . . . . . . . . . . 111
Pulborough, The Old House . . . . . . . . . . . . . . . . . . . . . . . . . 112
Robertsbridge. . . . . . . . . . . . . . . . . . . . . . . . . . . . . . . . . . . . . 113
Rye, Durrant House . . . . . . . . . . . . . . . . . . . . . . . . . . . . . . . . 114
Rye, Fletcher's House . . . . . . . . . . . . . . . . . . . . . . . . . . . . . . 115
Rye, St. Peter's House . . . . . . . . . . . . . . . . . . . . . . . . . . . . . . 116
Rye, The House Opposite . . . . . . . . . . . . . . . . . . . . . . . . . . . 117

*Bramber Castle Hotel, Bramber.*

Rye, The Flushing Inn . . . . . . . . . . . . . . . . . . . . . . . . . . . . . . . . . . . 118
Sharpthorne, Gravetye Manor Hotel, Restaurant & Country
    Club . . . . . . . . . . . . . . . . . . . . . . . . . . . . . . . . . . . . . . . . . . . . . . . 119
Shipley, The Old Cottage . . . . . . . . . . . . . . . . . . . . . . . . . . . . . . 120
Shoreham, Marlipins Museum . . . . . . . . . . . . . . . . . . . . . . . . . . 121
Slaugham . . . . . . . . . . . . . . . . . . . . . . . . . . . . . . . . . . . . . . . . . . . . 122
Southover, Priory of St. Pancreas . . . . . . . . . . . . . . . . . . . . . . 123
Southwick, The Schooner Inn . . . . . . . . . . . . . . . . . . . . . . . . . . . 124
Stanmer, The Stables, Stanmer House . . . . . . . . . . . . . . . . . . 125
Steyning, The Stone House . . . . . . . . . . . . . . . . . . . . . . . . . . . . . 126
Steyning, Grammar School . . . . . . . . . . . . . . . . . . . . . . . . . . . . . 127
Steyning, St. Andrew's Church . . . . . . . . . . . . . . . . . . . . . . . . . 128
Steyning, Springwells . . . . . . . . . . . . . . . . . . . . . . . . . . . . . . . . . 129
Stopham House . . . . . . . . . . . . . . . . . . . . . . . . . . . . . . . . . . . . . . . 130
Tarring, St. Andrew's Church . . . . . . . . . . . . . . . . . . . . . . . . . . 131
Upper Beeding . . . . . . . . . . . . . . . . . . . . . . . . . . . . . . . . . . . . . . . 132
Warnham, The Tower . . . . . . . . . . . . . . . . . . . . . . . . . . . . . . . . . 133
Wartling Hill, School Farm House . . . . . . . . . . . . . . . . . . . . . . 134
West Dean, Charleston Manor . . . . . . . . . . . . . . . . . . . . . . . . . . 135
West Grinstead, Bowshots House . . . . . . . . . . . . . . . . . . . . . . . 136
West Tarring, The Old Palace . . . . . . . . . . . . . . . . . . . . . . . . . . 137
West Hoathly, Priest House . . . . . . . . . . . . . . . . . . . . . . . . . . . . 138
West Hoathly, Manor House . . . . . . . . . . . . . . . . . . . . . . . . . . . 139
Wilmington, The Long Man of Wilmington . . . . . . . . . . . . . . 140
Wilmington Priory . . . . . . . . . . . . . . . . . . . . . . . . . . . . . . . . . . . . 141
Winchelsea, Strand Gate . . . . . . . . . . . . . . . . . . . . . . . . . . . . . . . 142
Wisborough Green, Sparr Farm . . . . . . . . . . . . . . . . . . . . . . . . . 143
Worthing, Steyne Gardens Church . . . . . . . . . . . . . . . . . . . . . . 144

# Aldingbourne

This mill house perfectly sums up Aldingbourne today as it is — a textbook Sussex country parish. Its mill equipment lies in retirement, overtaken by the years.

As indeed retirement overtook Oliver Cromwell, but not before his Roundheads had rampaged through the peace of Aldingbourne. The bishops set up their palace here about 1050 and probably converted a former monastery to do so.

Successive bishops were not backwards in lavishing improvements either and they won the "stayed here" badge of merit when King John himself stopped over for three days from Thursday, March 27, 1208.

King John concurred with the heavenly inspired choice of Aldingbourne. So much so that he came again the following year and again the following year and again in 1215.

But how times had changed when Civil War caught up with the populace and the Church. Some think it was because Bishop Roger Montague had upset the Parliamentarians' side by trying to bring England and Rome together again.

Upset them anyway someone certainly had, because in 1642 Parliamentary forces under Sir William Waller were marching from Chichester to Arundel after the siege of Chichester. And on the way they stopped off to knock the living daylights out of the bishops' country retreat! In fact they completely destroyed it and it is thought the cannibalised materials were later used for a farm building.

Aldingbourne Church has a story to tell us as well, a more peaceful one though because it is still standing. Its records show that after a 1681 order all people had to be buried wrapped in wool and that three people in the parish were thus interred, including the vicar — one Thomas Phillips, on August 1 of that year.

# Alfriston

Sussex coastal villages abound with tales of smuggling, and one of the most unusual originates from a 16th century beamed building, Moonrakers, in Alfriston.

About 200 years ago on a moonlit summer's evening, two smugglers were returning to Alfriston from Cuckmere Haven with barrels of contraband packed on their horses.

As they neared the village they heard a party of revenue officers approaching. The smugglers promptly sank the barrels of contraband into a nearby pond, and rode on past the officers unchallenged.

When they thought the coast was clear the smugglers returned to the pond armed with rakes to recover their loot.

But as they worked the revenue officers returned and asked what they were doing. The smugglers feigned ignorance and pointed to the moon reflected on the pond's surface.

They told the officers they were trying to rake out the cheese they could see floating on the water.

The revenue officers, convinced the smugglers were just ignorant peasants, laughed and moved on — leaving the moonrakers to recover their barrels.

# Alfriston

The impressive St. Andrew's in Alfriston is popularly regarded as the Cathedral of the Downs, and this 14th century church richly deserves the title.

It was built in about 1360 and, unlike many of its contemporaries, was built all at one time with no later additions.

The church is 115ft. long, 70ft. wide. It is thought that Poynings Church, built about the same time, was copied from Alfriston Church.

The site of the church is thought to date back to Saxon times, because there was a considerable Saxon community in the village before 1066.

But although the list of rectors goes back to at least 1272, there is no mention of the church in the Domesday Book of 1086.

The present church stands on a mound in the village green known as the Tye. Legend has it that the original intended site was to the west of the village street. But when work started the stones were mysteriously moved to the Tye.

Then villagers noticed four oxen lying together on the Tye in the shape of a cross, so they assumed divine providence thought better of a church there.

The church is built in the form of a Greek cross out of local flints, with greensand quoins and facings.

The flintwork is considered to be some of the finest in the country. The roof was originally covered with Horsham stone but this eventually proved to be too heavy and was replaced with tiles.

9

# Amberley

Stroll down any Sussex lane and you walk into history. But saunter down a street in the village of Amberley and you find a double helping of the past.

The cosy hamlet, sitting inland from Littlehampton, lies on a low ridge overlooking Amberley Wild Brooks.

It's a village where many houses boast thatched roofs. There is a castle built as a palace for the Bishops of Chichester around 1373 which luckily has never heard the clash of feuding parties.

A famous lover of the county once described trout caught in the nearby Arun as "one of the four good things of Sussex."

So there is history indeed, symbolised by Stream Cottage which sits snugly in the village square together with its neighbour, Forge Cottage.

Stream Cottage dates back to about 1587. Even the prominent box hedge in the garden is as least 300 to 400 years old.

The property is distinctive in more ways than one. One of the bedrooms has a head-knocking dwarf doorway and there's also a brick-built inglenock fireplace still boasting the original bread oven in a recess.

Forge Cottage doesn't stretch your imagination as to its original use. The village blacksmith toiled here and his predecessors before him, with a smithy in residence right up to 1955.

Thus the flavour of the past is preserved in street life. Nearby,

for instance, is Vine House, once a beer house and called the Golden Cross during the 18th century.

There's another home nearby called the Brew House, which is doubtless where the Golden Cross used to draw ale supplies.

Then there's the Bakehouse, with a name that tells of a rising past where two brothers, "Cosher" and "Jimmer" Allen, once kept Amberley supplied with bread.

Amberley Stores was a bakery too, and it belonged to James Cooter. Another owner emigrated to New Zealand, doubtless shaking hands before he did so with the occupier of Old Stack Cottage, one Mr. Short, who carried on the trade of shoe and harness maker.

AMBERLEY CASTLE

# Amberley

It isn't only the priceless gem of Chichester Cathedral we can thank Bishop Ralph de Luffa for.

The cathedral is grand, spiritually moving, and internationally famous.

The church at Amberley, for which this Norman bishop was also responsible, has similar timeless qualities.

First, and perhaps the key to its appeal, is age. The bishop himself lived from 1091 to 1123 and on the chancel walls outside the equally ancient church are indications of the original Norman apse, while the whole of the square front reflects the solid line of the period's architecture.

Inside are the remains of medieval wall paintings and above the pulpit, from which so many sermons have been preached through the generations, is an old iron hour glass stand that persumably once held the instrument of time to remind priests that even God's flock had their limits of listening patience.

But the times weren't always as peaceful as now. Next to the churchyard are the ruins of a castle that in its day was a fortified manor house for the bishops of Chichester.

It is thought the manor was bestowed on the bishops of Selsey, who were their predecessors, before the Normans clinched their invasion in 1066.

Some of the building's earliest work may be Norman but most of it dates from the 14th century.

Inside the castle is a picturesque house built in the 16th century by Bishop Sherborne, the last bishop to use the castle for a home.

But as with so much of the Sussex heritage, some of the castle's charm was destroyed when the men of Oliver Cromwell partly dismantled its outer walls during their Puritan days.

The castle itself stands on a low cliff facing the marshy stretches of Amberley Wild Brooks — Weald Brooks, in reality — which were probably a lake in medieval days.

The one thing Cromwell couldn't spoil was the beauty of the countryside in which the gem of Amberley is set.

# Angmering

Being a foreigner in England can be a taxing problem. But it used to be much more so — and literally. Edward III was the monarch to blame. He gave racial discrimination royal assent as a £SD money spinner and promptly taxed all foreign merchants here under a measure called "fifteenths."

At the time — around 1340 — a total of 65 such non-native milch cows lived in Sussex, and three of those in Angmering. One of those was called Thomas Pygeun, a Portuguese. All of which is a long-winded way of saying that he still had enough hard cash left to live in the delightful Pigeon House — one of the oldest buildings in the village.

Quite what brand of merchandise Mr P. traded in, history doesn't tell us. But the house it afforded him was a typical yeoman's home. It started off as a barn-like structure, a straight through affair with nothing ambitious like floors or chimneys. The smoke-blackened tie beam shows the kind of problems that followed.

Later, most probably in Tudor times, it was divided into two sections by an inner floor and had hearths installed. There were other extensions to the south in Cromwell's day. After the Pygeun occupation the Pigeon House pedigree becomes sketchy. Nothing more for sure is known until 1617 when it belonged to one Henry Gorringe, of Okehurst, Billingshurst. In 1753 it was sold by William Mitford, of Petworth, to Hugh Penfold, a yeoman of Angmering.

The farm buildings surrounding the Pigeon House are not without their merit and a barn was added in Tudor times. But the outhouse reputed to have interested an Australian wasn't so grand. Earlier this century it had been used as a garage and before that it was a labourer's hut, jokingly referred to as Angmering Hall. So laughs all round when the local vicar received an Aussie letter wanting to know about the Angmering Hall "stately" home he believed one of his ancestors had left behind as his heritage in Blighty.

# Appledram

Chichester lawyer William Ryman may have been through some heavy days helping justice along at the county town back in the early 1400s, but he certainly made sure of a posh place to go home to at the day's end.

Not surprisingly it became known as Rymans, a small ancient manor house of the most splendid proportions, and splendid age, which lies just outside Chichester at Appledram-Apuldram.

Mr Ryman had it built in 1412 and it has been added to over the years. The building consists of a three-storey central tower, with wings making an L-shape. The tower and one arm of the L remain despite a fire in 1964 when the house was unoccupied.

Rymans, though, was made of tough stuff in the form of stone brought over specially from the Isle of Wight and Normandy to Appledram-Apuldram.

It all came to a head in 1958 when Apuldrammers decided they wanted the village called Apuldram.

What that meant was, would West Sussex County Council, the Inland Revenue, Ordnance Survey, etc., please drop the nasty mordern spelling of Appledram?

But they didn't take it lying down at County Hall, not with the thought of roadsigns and the rest needing replacement.

So burrowing into maps and documents they eventually emerged triumphant with a 1600 map giving the Appledram spelling — and nothing older to contradict it.

At which point the parishioners went home defeated and the County Council were heard in whispers congratulating themselves on having won a Climping-Clymping victory over the teeniest trifle of olde worlde status-seeking.

They need not really have bothered. As William Ryman obviously found out. Appledram is a nice enough place to live before you start bothering what to call it.

# Ardingly

Sir Henry Price was a man whose life had style in two senses. He founded a money-spinning menswear empire called the Fifty Shilling Tailors, and he gave the nation the glories of Wakehurst Place, at Ardingly, with the profits.

Today the grounds of his former home are a mecca for greenfingered legions and famous as Kew in the country.

Sir Henry died in 1963 and left his home, together with £200,000, to the National Trust who in turn leased it to the Royal Botanical Gardens.

It was the horticultural peak of the times and the great gardener who helped make it so was botanist extraordinary Sir Gerald Loder earlier this century.

He bought Wakehurst in 1903, later became Lord Wakehurst before his death in 1937 and during his occupancy laid the foundations that make the gardens so famous today.

The 400-plus acres of woodlands are twice as big again as Kew and their value is that they are pollution free and give room for expansion. In Sussex there's not so much grime, the climate is kinder and the soil is better.

Hence the wonderland of rare shrubs and trees, the flower beds of Australasian and South American plants, the exotic blooms of the Himalayas and the big Californian redwoods.

The house was built by Sir Edward Culpepper in 1590. Before an earlier 11th century house had been owned for over 250 years by the Wakehurst family themselves.

But the Culpeppers didn't find everything in the garden rosy, and a Sir William Culpepper gambled away the family fortune and was forced to sell the family estate to a navy commissioner and a clerk of Chatham dockyard for the paltry sum of £9,000.

# Arundel

Christmas 1067 — Roger de Montgomery was created Earl of Arundel and given a third of Sussex.

It was a reward for his careful stewardship of Normandy while William was away conquering England.

Roger (probably) built the original motte and bailey castle at Arundel that has since become the ancestral home of the Dukes of Norfolk.

Arundel Castle thrived until the 14th earl, Thomas, left England at the outbreak of civil war in 1642.

During his absence the castle was besieged and sacked in 1643-8, and the Fitzalan Chapel desecrated by Parliamentary forces under the command of Sir William Waller.

The castle remained in ruins until the 18th century when Charles, the 11th duke and a personal friend of the Prince Regent began reconstruction.

Fourteenth duke, Henry Granville, continued reconstruction to the design of M. E. Hadfield but died before the work was completed.

His son, Henry turned instead to C. A. Buckler, the herald and antiquary, as his architect. Together they reconstructed and restored the castle between 1875 and 1900.

Arundel Castle was further extensively repaired by Messrs. Seely and Paget between 1975 and 1978, and is now vested in a special charitable trust to ensure its permanent preservation.

Maj. Gen. Miles Francis Stapleton Fitzalan Howard, 12th Lord Beaumont and fourth Lord Howard of Glossop is the 17th Duke of Norfolk.

15

# Arundel

Arundel Cathedral was founded by the 15th Duke of Norfolk and commissioned by him for his coming of age in 1868. It was first opened to worshippers in July 1873 and the architect concerned soon became a household name — but not for designing buildings. Joseph Aloysius Hansom became more famous, in fact, for his inventing the Hansom Cab.

The 15th Duke of Norfolk was a great admirer of Gothic architecture. He and the cathedral's builders, could think of no more superior position than the top of Parson's Hill, opposite the walls of Arundel Castle, as the cathedral's site but it was far from perfect in other respects. To support the 280ft, spire, foundations had to be sunk more than 50ft, into the hillside. Even with that precaution, emergency work has had to be carried out to prevent sinking of the cathedral's marble floor.

When built, the building was soon noted for its geometrically shaped windows — especially the wheel window at the west end. The founder duke often worshipped there, sometimes sitting quietly and unnoticed in the back pews.

16

# Arundel

The Arundel Emporium in Tarrant Street, Arundel, came near to disaster in 1927 when a fire swept towards its high brick walls.

The design made the Victorian warehouse — type building particularly vulnerable. But fortunately the fire by-passed it and carried on, leaving the Emporium untouched.

The property was built in 1877 by architect and designer Charles Sparkes, and on one side of the building his original sign still remains.

When it was built, the Arundel Emporium was used as an auction house, and for storage. The building later passed into the hands of George Sparkes, the architect's son, who continued to use it for auctions. He also incorporated an upholstery and piano rental business there.

Later the building declined. It was fully restored in 1977 when it was bought by James Cartland, who converted it into ten shops, offices and flats.

# Arundel

It is hard to believe, looking at elegant No. 10 in Maltravers Street, Arundel, that once all that remained of the building was a single chimney surrounds by smoking ruins.

The original house, believed to date back to the 16th century, was razed to the ground by Cromwell's forces. The shelling took place over several days, and eventually all they left was the chimney and fireplace.

But in Queen Anne's time the house was completely rebuilt around the fireplace, and now stands as one of Arundel's most distinguished properties.

The house has another reminder of the past; part of the old town wall of Arundel still stands in the garden.

The house once belonged to the Duke of Norfolk, and was sold for £200 to help pay the costs of the duke's estates.

The exterior is of Flemish brickwork, but inside is one of the most interesting aspects of the house — a secret tunnel, which is reputed to lead to the castle and is thought to have been built during the Civil War.

As recently as the turn of the century, the house was a pub, called the Black Bull.

# Ashurst

St. Cuthman had more than an eye for just spiritual values all those centuries ago.

He also knew how to spot earthly corners that had scenic heavenly virtues — which is why he is reputed to have lived at Ashurst, a tiny village lost in greenery near Steyning.

Whether he knew Blocques we ourselves do not know. Certainly he would have liked to.

This yeoman-style country house traces its history back to at least 1556, the farthest point in the past the present owners have managed to trace it.

They think the main part of their home may once have been an ancient hall, detective work borne out by smokeblackened roof timbers discovered by an archaeologist.

Most of the house now seems certain to date from Tudor times, but the original Horsham slab roof has been replaced by tiles.

Saints aren't the only people who have been hereabouts. The military have been through too, and left minus a load of brass buttons.

A large amount of them saw the light of day again recently when a history sleuth with a metal detector came to Blocques.

Experts who examined them concluded that they must have been left by a company of soldiers stationed here and the buttons eventually ended up at a museum.

Blocques was not always so namewise. It used to be called Blocks, a much more English spelling and probably one dating back to an original Saxon title.

The French variation came about thanks to the expansionist French church. They were around in the form of the Abbey of Fecamp and the church at Ashurst, once a small chantry owned by them.

The present church dates from around 1200 and was built by the Knights Templar.

Along with Blocques it couldn't look more English today despite past connections.

# Balcombe

You would have felt the same if you had been a pilgrim in the Middle Ages and had just seen two yew trees.

Imagine the sweat and struggle of it all. Canterbury is many trudging miles away. Your leather sandals are taxing both sorts of souls, and the local peasants are probably too busy scratching a living to accord you acknowledgement of a pilgrim's progress.

To spot two yews then must have had the value almost of a religious miracle. In brief it meant: lay-by ahead, brother — food, water and lodgings here.

Such relief would have been yours on approaching the White House at Balcombe. Once it was a house run by the white friars and many of its guests were Canterbury pilgrims.

But it took a garden expert who toured the grounds recently to explain the yew tree coding to the property's owners.

The trees were planted on high standing ground to point the way to such friendly places as the White House. Two yews still there are reminders of that spiritual signpost era.

The years, as well as the footsore monks, have passed. Now this stylish property has moved into more secular realms.

Much of it dates back to the 13th century, including ancient walls filled with animal dung as insulation. A building is reputed to have stood on the site even before the 13th century.

But it was Lutyens in 1909 who changed the building from a house of God into a house of upper class prosperity when he superivsed extensive restoration work.

# Battle

The people of Battle love their local workhouse. They arrange dances to raise cash for it, organise darts matches to earn it yet more money, and generally hold a dear place in their hearts for the fabled institution.

It's not so strange as you'd think, though. For today the workhouse is a comfy, well equipped hospital for old people and a valued asset of the local society, its stigma of old well and truly buried in the past.

It was in the early 1800s that Battle Hospital first took in its down-on-their luck guests.

Then it was one of a chain of such workhouses that stretched through Sussex giving basic accommodation and food for the numerous poor and distressed of those less affluent times.

The civic authorities of those days worked on the principle of providing basic bed and breakfast for the vagrant drifters wandering the country, preferably sited on high ground so that the guests could see these distinctive halfway hostels.

Battle's offering is stonebuilt, with an entrance drive going stately-style under an archway and into a courtyard for dis-embarkation.

After its early years as a workhouse, the building became a local infirmary, mostly for the chronic sick, old people and maternity cases.

It became a hospital exclusively for old people about 13 years ago.

Now the 60 patients live in relative VIP style. The hospital has recently been improved and updated, and has more facilities than the first residents could ever have dreamed of.

The building is recognised as being of historic importance and, as such, the Government has listed it as a property among those with a history and a past worth preserving.

Doubtless, the first clients would have had a selection of choice ironic sayings if they could have foreseen such a lofty fate for a place with such humble beginnings.

# Billingshurst

Fossil hunters can examine first rate examples while sipping cocktails at the Jennie Wren restaurant in Billingshurst.

Slabs of Sussex marble covered with fossil markings, mainly shells, form the stone floor of the cocktail bar.

The restaurant is in Groomsland House, a building — dating back to 1480 — which has been a farm for most of its history.

Several years ago it became the Great Groomes restaurant but was closed in 1970 and the building remained empty for a year.

In 1971 Denis and Jennie Tilbury bought the house and have since knocked down walls and made the interior more spacious.

They decided to call it the Jennie Wren, but kept Groomsland in the title of the house as a name peculiar to the property.

As well as the unusual fossil floor, the building boasts an almost intact bread oven inglenook fireplace.

Three fireplaces once fed the chimney stack — which has a small priest's hiding place — but now the only remaining fireplace is in the dining room.

Groomsland house has a hand-made clay tile roof, and stands in a third of an acre of land. Vegetables grown in the garden are served in the restaurant.

# Birling Gap

One of the most popular families in Sussex are the Seven Sisters who make up a spectacular part of the county's coastline.

These white chalk cliffs rise from the sea west of Birling Gap, near Eastbourne.

Not all of the sisters have feminine names. The first is known as West Hill Brow. She is 146ft high and is the end of an ancient ridge heading north-west along the edge of the Downs into Hampshire and Wiltshire.

The next sister along is called Bailey's Hill and towers 194ft, over the English Channel. Then comes Flagstaff Point, 153ft.; Bran Point 160ft.; Rough Brow 216ft.; Show Brow, 180ft; and, head and shoulders above all the others, Haven Brow at 255ft.

At Haven Brow are the foundations of a tiny Saxon church where a light used to warn mariners about dangerous rocks.

But the silent sisters have seen many ships wrecked beneath them. At Flagstaff Point in 1747 a Spanish vessel met its end and villagers came from miles around to rob the wreck.

They were so intent on getting home with their purloined booty that they didn't bother to help the ship's luckless crew.

One Lewes man is said to have taken so much plunder that he was able to build himself a mansion at Seaford with the proceeds.

A barn was built from the ship's wreckage and legend says that 30 wagonloads of silver each valued at £800 were trundled up the Sussex coast to go beneath the floorboards of greedy villagers.

# Bodiam

There's a castle at Bodiam, up in East Sussex towards the Kent border and in the green and pleasant valley of the Rother. Just a glimpse of its gaunt, weather-worn remains is enough to fix it in the memory as one of the most romantic and picturesque ruins in the county.

From a moat that is covered with a green carpet of water lilies in summer, its four-square, bluff, grey walls rise up in a majesty that has brought splendour to the countryside hereabouts since the 14th century.

As for the manor of Bodiam itself, it passed to Sir Edward Dalyngrigge, a knight who had honourably acquited himself in the French wars and in the 1385 he was given permission to "crenellate" or fortify his manor house.

And so it was that the castle came to be built on a hill overlooking the Rother and doubtless sited so that it controlled the river, which in those days was navigable up to Bodiam Bridge.

But for all its bluff indestructible appearance, the castle has never really been put to the test. In the War of the Roses it came into the hands of Sir Thomas Lewknor, who fell foul of Richard III for backing the Yorkists. The Earl of Surrey was sent hotfoot to lay siege to Bodiam, but the defenders gave in without much of a struggle.

It next fell to the Parliamentarians to partly dismantle it during the Civil War — possible after a siege. During the centuries after, the castle had various owners, but none so caring as the Marquess of Curzon who bought it in 1917, restored the ruins and bequeathed them to the National Trust.

As for the splendid architecture of the castle, its walls are more than 6ft. thick in some places and tower 41ft. above the moat. For sheer impact, the entrance gatehouse is probably one of the most impressive in England — with two rectangular towers over 60ft. in height crowned by parapets and joined by a lofty arch.

Certainly it's safe to say that not every Englishman is lucky enough to have a home life this castle.

# Bolney

Pinch–and–look–again architecture — that's the bracket Wykehurst Park falls into.

Disneyland is one thing, German fairy princess castles another, but this is Bolney, UK — the heart of Sussex.

The magnificent 105-room mansion is about as grandiose a flight of fancy as taste and cash will allow. It's like the product of a hybrid meeting between a French chateau and a Rhineland schloss — all towers, pinnacles, turrets and windows.

The original creator was Henry Huth, the son of a German banker who purchased the 144 acres specially to have his dream home built.

Architect was Edward Middleton Barry, the son of Sir Charles Barry, and the builders were the William Cubit company, who also built Osborn House for Queen Victoria.

It was in 1871 that work started. Three years later, and at the absurd price of £35,000, it was finished.

An antique looking building it may be today, but by building standards of those times its construction methods were nothing short of revolutionary.

The Victorian advanced technology included some of the first cavity walls used in such a massive structure fire-proof floors of iron and concrete, an efficient hot water supply to the three floors and main rooms heated by ducted warm air.

But the high standards had one inevitable companion, high cost. Running Wykehurst Park proved too much when Victorian wealth began to dry up.

Sixty-five years after it was built the majestic house stood empty and time, plus the elements, struck at the heart of the fabric.

For 32 years the corridors echoed only to lonely mice and the dusty footsteps of memory.

Apart from troops billeted there during the war, Wykehurst slept the sleep of abandonment.

# Bramber

Lovers' tunnels may have been great exercise for the diggers. But when it came to usage for the original love purpose they could pose tricky problems in the days of old.

Take the one supposed to have led from Bramber Castle to a summer house in the grounds of Lavender Cottage, today a restaurant in busy Bramber.

The cottage dates back to the 15th century, so you can guess there are tales for the telling.

The tunnel was reputed to have been an amorous underground love route for a young man at the castle, to enable him to swap its grim and fortified battlement for the much softer and sweeter pleasures of a waiting young lady.

But, obviously, either she wasn't free from marital bonds or someone else with a romantic interest took a dim view of it all.

The outcome, says documented legend, is that a foul trap was laid. The offended party lay in wait, pounced on the castle lover in his tunnel and promptly bricked him up to suffer a horrid, lingering death in a damp Bramber tomb.

The history of Lavender Cottage, which rests in two acres of grounds, can be traced back to medieval times.

Then it was a fisherman's home in the days when the sea came up to Bramber before retreating to Shoreham.

Another victim of the years, of course, was Bramber Castle itself, and some of the beams from this historic fortress are reputed to have been incorporated in the cottage.

Its use as a cafe and guesthouse dates back for about 60 years.

Its future as another interesting and rewarding Sussex building is guaranteed.

*Gerald Lip*

# Brighton

In the run-up to the Royal Wedding, Brighton doesn't have far to look for a link with the Prince of Wales.

The Royal Pavilion, with its oriental domes and minarets, was created by George Augustus Frederick, Prince of Wales, and later Prince Regent and King George IV.

The building was originally known as Brighton House, and was a gentleman's farmhouse by the sea. But in 1787 the prince commissioned the architect Henry Holland to transform it into a classical villa with a central rotunda and north and south wings.

Prinny's fascination with the Orient ensured that from 1802 onwards vast sums were spent rebuilding and enlarging the Royal Pavilion.

Today's Pavilion is mostly the work of John Nash, the architect of Regent's Park and Carlton House Terrace.

After 1845 it became clear that the Government wanted to sell the Pavilion and its grounds so they could be redeveloped. But a residents' petition raised £53,000 to save the building.

The Pavilion has not always been praised. William Hazlitt called it "a collection of stone pumpkins and pepper boxes". William Cobbett added it reminded him of the Kremlin.

Fortunately the public began to appreciate the building and in the 1930s it was carefully restored.

Today the building that was once described as "Prinny's Folly" now stands as the fourth most popular tourist attraction in Britain.

# Brighton

The future has never looked brighter for Volk's Railway. The single-track line along Brighton seafront has been on the right track since it opened in August 1883 — the first electric railway in Britain.

Not long ago it had its own mini-Beeching crisis when the council considered moving it to an inland park or dismantling it completely.

But along came the marina and lots of obliging tourists. Now it looks as if the signals are permanently on go.

Magnus Volk would have been pleased.

He was the inventor and the first driver of the railway, which hurtled down the track at a breathtaking six miles per hour.

But that, said opponents, would scare the horses. And others muttered that electricity was the work of the Devil.

The council weren't so short-sighted but they weren't optimistic either. They gave him the go-ahead to run the service to the Old Chain Pier, but wanted everything removed from the beach by summer's end — when they though the five-minute wonder would be over.

Yet in three months 20,000 people had travelled as passengers on the railway.

The following year was even better. The line was extended and in the first six months 200,000 passengers were carried.

Carriages were lavishly equipped with engraved plate glass windows and panelled ceilings, decorated with hand-painted blue flowers and gilt mouldings.

The railway wasn't Volk's only stroke of genius.

This man of invention was the first Englishman to export an electric car.

His home in Preston Drove was the first to have electric light plus a private telephone to his works and friends. He also put electricity in the Royal Pavilion and invented an automatic device for turning over the pages of printed music.

# Brighton

The Old Ship Hotel in Brighton is not only the oldest hotel in the town, but has also featured in its most exciting episode — the flight of Charles II to France.

Fleeing after a defeat by the Roundheads at Worcester, Charles and a few of his followers took refuge in the George Inn, West Street.

Here they contacted a local seaman, Captain Nicholas Tettersell, who agreed to smuggle two unknown men to France in his cargo ship the Surprise.

She was on her way from Newcastle to Poole with a cargo of coal and that night was beached at Shoreham.

Tettersell is alleged to have said on meeting the King for the first time: "I think I do God and my country good service in preserving the King, and by the grace of God I will venture my life and set him safely on shore in France."

At dawn the next morning the small party of men boarded the Surprise at Shoreham. Tettersell first made course for the Isle of Wight, but as soon as he was out of sight of land he sailed towards the French coast.

On October 15 the Surprise sailed into the tiny fishing village

of Fecamp, which marked the beginning of Charles II's ten-year exile.

When the King was restored the Surprise was renamed the Royal Escape and its captain was granted a commission by the Royal Navy. He was also given an annuity, with which he bought the Old Ship Tavern — now the Old Ship Hotel.

Even today Captain Tettersell is not forgotten and his picture hangs in the cocktail lounge, alongside that of Charles II, the Royal Escape and the original document granting Tettersell the annuity.

# Brighton

Brighton's Theatre Royal in New Road started life in Duke Street.

But soon after the turn of the 18th century the owner, Hewitt Cobb, closed the Duke Street theatre to build a larger one opposite the Pavilion.

The original transfer deed bears the signature of the Prince of Wales, under whose patronage the foundation stone was laid on September 10, 1806.

The first performance took place there on June 27 the following year, with Mr and Mrs Kemble appearing in Hamlet.

In 1866 the Cobb family sold the theatre to Mr Henry Nye Chart, an actor-manager. In true theatrical style he married his leading lady, who assumed control of the theatre after his death.

By the 1880s Mrs Chart's local stock company was replaced by touring shows and the theatre's prestige soared.

Despite numerous alterations and modernisations, the building has retained its charm over the years.

The colonnade of plain round columns were added in about 1894, when the building also had electric lighting installed.

It is one of the best known theatres in the South, and a host of international stars have appeared there.

# Brighton

The people of Regency Square in Brighton have always had strong feelings about the nearby West Pier.

Today, many of them are trying to stop it from being demolished — but when the pier was built in 1866 they would have been happy to see it dismantled.

They felt the pier and its toll houses obscured their view of the sea.

Prior to the square's construction in 1818 the land was known as Belle Vue Field.

Up until 1807 the field was used for fairs and shows, but shortly after that it was bought by Joshua Hanson. He intended to build a square and call it Waterloo Square, but delays meant the square was not laid out until 1818, so he decided to call it Regency Square.

The house with the most interesting history in Regency Square is No. 1, originally Regency House.

In July 1830 it was bought by the Duke and Duchess of St. Albans as their Brighton residence. Harriot Mellon, the duchess, had one of the most remarkable careers in the 18th century.

She was the illegitimate daughter of a wardrobe keeper in an Irish theatrical company, and became a successful actress. In 1815 she married elderly banker Thomas Coutts, who died seven years later at the age of 87 and bequeathed his entire fortune to her.

At the age of 45, Mrs Coutts found herself the richest woman in England, and was courted from every side. Among those seeking her company was the ninth Duke of St. Albans, who was just 21.

She discouraged him at first because of the difference in their ages, but in 1827 they married, and after that visited Brighton almost every season.

They held huge parties in their Regency Square home, which had gigantic stables and a riding school attached.

The riding school was, with the exception of Westminster Abbey, the largest room in England whose roof was not supported by pillars, and the dome surrounding the stables rivalled St. Paul's in size.

Both these buildings were unfortunately demolished after the war.

# Brighton

The sweeping seafront Royal Crescent was one of the first roads in Kemp Town to be completed.

West Indian speculator J.B. Otto bought the land for this work of Regency grandeur in 1799, when only a stray cottage or windmill could be found east of Rock Gardens. It was almost never finished — only six houses had been built when Mr Otto ran out of money. The final houses were not completed until 1807.

The result is an interesting combination of architectural styles, but all the 14 houses have classical doorways, ironwork balconies and black "mathematical" tiles which help to protect the buildings from the driving winds and spray that go with a seafront view.

Mr Otto hoped that his investment would win him the favour of the Prince Regent and an invitation to the glittering functions at the Pavilion. He even commissioned a plaster statue of the Prince in the uniform of the Colonel of the 10th Hussars.

The result, standing seven feet high on a ten-feet pedestal, appeared on the lawn in front of Royal Crescent just after the final houses were ready. But the artifical stone that the sculptor Rossi had used didn't stand up to the climate. The Prince's right arm was blown off by a gale and his nose, cloak and left hand quickly disintegrated.

The statue was often mistaken for one of Lord Nelson, and Mr Otto became the laughing stock of Brighton . . . and never got past the door of the Pavilion.

His statue was removed in 1819, but the houses in Royal Crescent have stood the test of time and given pleasure to thousands of visitors to Brighton, as well as attracting some famous residents — including Lord Olivier, who lived in two of the converted houses until 1976.

# Brighton

Grand is an appropriate name for that famous Brighton seafront hotel. Brightonians may take this Victorian palace by the sea for granted. But next time you are passing its elegant facade remember the building's vital statistics.

There are 3½ million bricks; 12,500 cubic feet of York and Portland stone; 450 tons of wrought and cast iron; 30 miles of flooring; 15 miles of wallpaper; and 1½ acres of glazed tiles.

It was in December 1862 that the first stone in this nine-storey hotel was laid. Nineteen hectic months later 300 bedrooms opened to the first enthusiastic guests.

Nightly charges for bedrooms ranged from 2s 6d on the top floor to £1 10s on the first floor. Hot and cold baths would have set you back an extra 1s, with additional pails of hot or cold seawater an extra 6d. Keeping warm was costly, though. The luxury of a fire in the bedroom cost 1s 6d, and a hip bath and night light were 6d each.

A steak and vegetables cost 2s and, in the opening week, oysters were 1s a dozen, with sandwiches 6d each. A choice of 200 wines was on offer.

The sculptor who gave the Grand such a distinctive Italian facade was one Adam Gamle, who wrought similar magic on the Houses of Parliament and Buckingham Palace.

# Brighton

Ever heard of Fred Robertson of Brighton?

His uniquely human story was acted out on the stage of Holy Trinity, the Brighton town centre church in Ship Street that thousands pass and yet few take notice of.

Mr Robertson was born in 1816 and his was a military family. Both his father and grandfather were proud soldiers.

He wanted to follow into the ranks — until a holiday spiritual awakening in the Tyrol turned his eyes towards religion and his heart towards God.

After Oxford he was ordained by the Bishop of Winchester in 1840 and was a curate in that city and in Cheltenham.

Perhaps it was here, by what a later Archbishop of Canterbury called "a selfish, comfortable individualism" that the fires of reaction were stoked.

Certainly, when Fred Robertson arrived in Brighton to take over the Holy Trinity Church in 1847, he was no cosy, conservative, establishment vicar.

Fred Robertson began to fill the church to overflowing every time he gave a sermon.

So eloquent, so compassionate were his words thousands flocked to listen.

Books of his sermons began to appear, to proliferate. He became known simply as Fred Robertson of Brighton, and the publishing wave grew even wider.

His words reached countless nations throughout the Western world and especially in America. Millions were parishioners at his services.

The pity was that they never reached the stony hearts of Brighton's establishments. For Fred Robertson was a teacher who stepped on the toes of Mammon.

In 1848 he took part in the founding of the Brighton Working Men's Institute.

# Brighton/Hove

There couldn't have been more fuss about unveiling what has become known as the Peace Statue on the Brighton and Hove seafront boundary in 1912. The only trouble was that war broke out two years later.

It wasn't exactly the statue's fault though. The intentions there were fine enough. The good people of Brighton and Hove wanted to pay tribute to the late King Edward VII, a frequent Sussex coast visitor, and they also wanted to help out the Queen's Nurses as well.

What better way then was there to do it than a public subscription for a statue, with a hefty percentage going to a new nurses' home in Wellington Road that, like the statue, is still standing today.

And so it all came to pass. A competition was held to design the most fitting memorial. The winning entry came from young Chelsea sculptor, Mr Newbury Trent, and a striking one it was too.

The statue is a female figure standing over 30ft high, holding in one hand an olive branch, in the other an orb and facing north with wings poised.

The cost of it all was £1,000, even in those days, and the nurses came in for £2,000. So it was worth all the pomp and ceremony of the unveiling ceremony in October 1912.

It was a bright autumn day and the whole area was cordoned off. Obviously the ceremony was performed by the then Duke of Norfolk and there to help him were the Brighton Municipal Chorus singing the National Anthem, the Territorials, the 50th Brigade of the Royal Artillery, the Sussex Yeomanry and the Bishop of Chichester with his prayer of dedication.

Off came the wraps on the dedication which said then, as now: "In the year 1912 the inhabitants of Brighton and Hove provided a home for the Queen's Nurses and erected this monument in memory of King Edward VII".

# Burgess Hill

It may have been a "miserable world" that Sir Edward Michelborne left and which he described as such in his will of 1609. But he didn't take the heavenly exit road without first having a handsomely adventurous bite at it.

Edward lived in the rural splendour of Hammonds Place, at Burgess Hill. That's when he was at home, which wasn't often.

He swapped the relative calm of Sussex for Cathay, China, Japan and Korea when he obtained the King's licence to discover the countries and to trade with people living there.

He set out on his journeys in 1604 in a boat appropriately called The Tiger — his family crest. Yet by all accounts it was not so much trade by barter as acquisition by sword that Sir Edward achieved.

There are records of his plundering a Chinese ship and generally being more than forceful — with the obvious consequent legend of fabled treasure buried under the flower-beds of Hammonds Place.

He got his name on the East India Company's charter in 1600, where it stayed until he became mixed up in an earl's rebellion and was disenfranchised the next year.

When he became disenfranchised of life itself he gave many gifts to his children and servants but couldn't resist a parting shot at the Earl of Dorset, who in his will he stated owed him money.

The house which was the backcloth to Sir Edward's colourful life is said to have been known in Elizabethan days as A-Woods. It was probably added to by Sir Edward's father, another Edward, and it is his initials EM that can still be seen above the doorway.

Needless to say Queen Elizabeth I is supposed to have stayed here.

# Burpham

The present villagers of Burpham aren't the first to take a liking to the place. The Saxons were there and they established a burgh or fortified township, one of many thought to have been set up by Alfred the Great to ward off attacks by the Danes.

What fortifies Burpham these days is countryside, lots of green, rolling fields and a single lane which leads to this charming village on the banks of the Arun near Arundel.

And what best represents it and its idyllic setting is Burpham church. The building is of mixed period contributions. People were worshipping on the site before the Normans came and a church is mentioned in the Domesday Book.

The present building actually has parts dating from those times incorporated in what is now mostly a 12th and 13th century structure.

The nave is late Norman with unusual piers and an arcade of chalk with carved capitals and zigzag mouldings.

The church typifies the sense of history that lies thick on the ground in Burpham. Nearby is one of the largest and best known earthworks in Sussex. It measures 317 impressive yards in length and goes up to seven yards high.

Local historians have guessed that it was erected to protect early Burpham inhabitants from possibly less friendly people who might have cast longing eyes on this sheltered spot.

In those times it was surrounded by water on three other sides and constituted a more than formidable buffer.

History has come galloping through Burpham as well as growing up here. Charles II rode through the village after being beaten at the Battle of Worcester and while on his way to Shoreham and eventual escape to France.

Today's visitors should take more time to enjoy such an English pleasure.

BURPHAM CHURCH

# Bury

Bury House is just the place to write about — or in. Certainly novelist and poet John Galsworthy found the latter to be true because he lived here from 1926 until 1933.

The fond stories that have been told about this famous storyteller are many. The Forsyte Saga was completed here, for a start, and other famous authors were visitors.

But Galsworthy is chiefly remembered for his kindness.

On arrival he double the wages of all five gardeners. He loaned £100 to a Bury villager in trouble over a debt and, when the villager faithfully repaid it, gave the cash back again as a gift.

Then he heard about a Bury lorry driver who had been killed in a road accident. Galsworthy bought the widow her cottage so that she could live rent free. He bought eight other cottages too, fitting them out with bathrooms. When residents became worried about increasing rents, the author promptly reduced them!

Galsworthy first heard about his Nobel Prize for literature while playing a game of croquet at Bury House.

He had bought the property after falling in love with this part of the country.

The reproduction, 22-bedroomed manor house, with grey stone, mullion windows, and a slab roof, on the site of an earlier house destroyed by fire, cost him £9,000.

He lived here with his wife Ada, nephew Ruda Gauter and his wife Vi.

When he died, his ashes were scattered on Bury Hill in accordance with instructions found on a single piece of paper in his study: "Scatter my ashes! Let them be free to the air". Those of his wife were also scattered here when she died 22 years later.

# Chailey

They were called friendly societies, the earliest forerunners of today's insurance companies. And friendly they must have seemed in the harsher times before the Welfare State.

But just imagine any insurance company meeting with the sort of rules that were in force when the first friendly society in Sussex held its gatherings at the Five Bells, Chailey.

The first recorded get together of the Chailey Friendly Society was in 1782 and it was set up to provide relief in sickness, infirmity and old age for all members and their widows.

They met quarterly, in the winter from five to eight p.m., and in the summer from seven until 10 p.m.

That was when they used to bring into effect a set of rules which put a strict face on friendliness. The price to each member for food and drink at such meetings was ninepence, a princely sum in those days.

It was the steward's duty, as laid down in rules still preserved at the Five Bells, to ensure that the food and drink was of "the requisite and good quality". The rules also stipulated that if the publican didn't meet the standards set he had to forfeit five shillings.

Things weren't so princely in the original days of the pub. It goes back to around 1490, and was originally a yeoman's cottage attached to a nearby manor house.

The name Five Bells is thought to derive from the number of times the Chailey church bells were rung regularly. Once they were pealed seven times — then the pub was called the Seven Bells.

# Chichester

After the Norman conquest William ordered that all cathedrals be moved from small villages to more important centres.

In 1075 the see of Chichester was established in what had been a major Roman site. Bishop Ralph de Luffa then began to build the cathedral.

Work was hindered by fire in 1114 but went on throughout the 12th century, and the cathedral was finally consecrated by Bishop Seffrid in 1184.

Three years later fire ravaged the building, particularly damaging the east end.

It seems that those who rebuilt the cathedral sometimes used the old stone which had been weakened by the heat.

This is one of the reasons for the structural weaknesses now proving so expensive nearly 800 years later.

The stone vault was added later and enormously increased the weight and outward thrust on the walls.

Flying buttresses were also added on the outside, as well as the shafts from roof to floor inside, and the walls were thickened.

The building was reconsecrated in 1199. Chapels on either side of the nave were added in the 13th century and this made the

combined nave, aisles and chapels wider than any other English cathedral except York Minster.

Currently Chichester Cathedral faces two structural problems, and work is underway to remedy both.

The first is that over a period of years the outside ground level has been raised, allowing water to drain in under the building, causing movement in the structure.

And secondly, time and atmosphere have seriously eroded the stonework of the central tower and spire.

# Chichester

Visionary and mystic William Blake might have less than fond memories of the Grey Friars Chancel at Chichester if he were here today.

This splendid piece of religious architecture, which has survived the ravages of time, has also known secular use. At one period it was functioning as a court and it was here that Blake stood trial on a malicious treason charge, brought by a soldier after the poet had thrown him from the garden of a cottage he was living in at nearby Felpham.

That was in the early 1800's, by which time the chancel was already the most senior of buildings. It was built between 1270 and 1280 on a site given to the Grey Friars for a dwelling by Richard, Earl of Cornwall.

The Friars were dissolved in 1538 and in 1541 the building, in the heart of Chichester, was granted to the mayor and citizens of the city as a quick piece of municipal advantage taking.

It was they who converted the chancel into a guildhall, a building for the conducting of public affairs, in 1541 and as a shire hall it was later used for assizes until 1748 and for election counts until 1888.

# Chiddingly

Cobwebs cottage at Chiddingly takes the name from its inglenook fireplace. Smoke from logs burnt on the fire caused a never ending supply of cobwebs in the lounge of the 400-year-old house.

The cottage is dated at around 1585 by a Queen's pinion in the roof timbers. This was only used in late 16th century.

There are original oak beams throughout the house, and a large chunk cut out of one indicates where the grandfather clock once stood.

An 1821 census of Chiddingly shows that Cobwebs was then two cottages known as Tygers House, Hale.

It is known that in the late 18th century a woman called Mrs Gorringe lived in one of the cottages.

She used to cure bacon, as is testified by a meat hanging hook on one of the beams and a worn-down stone outside the front door where she sharpened her knife.

# Climping

Bailiffscourt, Climping, three miles from Littlehampton, was built 60 years ago at a cost of about £1 million. It must stand as one of the most expensive follies ever.

It might also qualify as one of the most outrageous fakes ever, were it not built almost entirely from bits of genuine old house . . . presumably making it a genuine fake!

Its strange story began in the 1920s when Lord Moyne bought a 1,000 acre stretch of land bordering the sea. On the estate there was a derelict Norman chapel and a Georgian farmhouse bordering a moat.

Lord Moyne appointed Amayas Phillips, the antiquarian and authority on medieval architecture, to restore it. Phillips was given a free hand and a blank cheque.

He first demolished the farmhouse, and found hundreds of pieces of stone from the original 12th century buildings embedded in the wall.

There were not enough to restore the buildings fully, so Phillips and his men scoured the country for stone and timber from demolished buildings.

Stone arches were found in a priory, a moulded oak ceiling came from an outbuilding attached to a rectory and a 15th century door with its original lock came to light in a Somerset stable.

When Phillips realised the site had no trees he uprooted two whole woods on the Downs — and transported them to the site.

The Norman chapel standing not far from the house has also been restored. It was used in the past as a dairy, a cellar — and a maid's bedroom.

# Cooden Beach

History sleuths Mr and Mrs Norman Ward Jones tracked down the ancient records of Barnhorne Manor at Cooden Beach, near Bexhill, after a long and patient search.

A countess once sold the records to an American university, so when Mr and Mrs Ward Jones were in the States on holiday they rounded of a 6,000 mile journey with a special visit to the campus to find out more about their home.

The only trouble was the univeristy was shut for the vacation. But a few brief words with the curator, a touch of American hospitality and courtesy, and the exhibits were soon opened up — revealing an English history right back to King Offa in 772.

There is a relatively "recent" lease on Barnhorne dating from 1494, left by the monks of yesteryear.

When they lived at Barnhorne they kept meticulous lists and accounts.

The records show what they had for dinner, the taxes they reaped on land owned and which monks were down for flower changing duties on what days.

Mr and Mrs Ward Jones had copies of the ancient records made and sent back to the county centre at Lewes for the sake of our pride and national heritage.

Long ago the manor of Barnhorne was a civic centre of some importance. An adjoining courthouse — now gone — functioned to sort out felons and criminals.

The monks themselves had later need of law when the manor was taken away from them not long after the Conquest. They launched a legal battle to have their lands returned and in 1120 they went to court and after a three-day hearing won their property — and the manor — back.

Today the manor's early 13th century architecture contains welcome simplicity. In essence the house is just a collection of rooms around a central chimney, a design which one old lease describes as "a house with three halves".

# Cooksbridge

John Davis hung up his stone-mason's chisel 22 years ago to take over the Rainbow Inn at Cooksbridge, near Lewes.

Now he's turned this historic building into a thriving country pub and restaurant and well and truly carried on the wishes of John Henderson, a predecessor.

Henderson started the pints flowing in this quiet corner of Sussex by embarking on what today would be called an aggressive programme of business expansion.

On October 11, 1830, he put an advertisement in a newspaper called the Sussex Advertiser in which he told an eager rural world of his intention to branch out and stretch his existing village shop into a public house which over the years has grown into the Rainbow.

The advert must have made cheering reading in those thirsty days before the beer can brought booze to the freezer.

Mr Henderson promised the sale of genuine beer, ales, porter, cider and ginger beer to be served in the best of surroundings and with promptness spiced with civility.

Forecasting the whims of public taste was obviously something Mr Henderson had plenty of experience at.

He had been a shopkeeper in Cooksbridge for 40 years and was plainly an expert on early consumer marketing trends.

The proprietor has no idea how the pub acquired its name and the source of it is lost in the misty past — a past that goes back at least to 1749, as a garden sundial complete with date indicates.

# Cowbeech

The year is 1731. John Kay is about to invent the flying shuttle and revolutionise the textile industry. Jethro Tull is on the verge of publishing the Horse–Hoing Husbandry, advocating new methods of agriculture. And Frederick the Great is not far off becoming king of Prussia.

Meanwhile, back in the heart of Sussex, Cowbeech House at Cowbeech was finished and ready for occupation.

Measured against the backcloth of history, that might not be thought much of an event.

But history is made up as much of the domestic as the dramatic, and down in this part of Sussex east of Lewes the completion of this fine traditional country mansion must have been a day to celebrate.

The house is scheduled as a Grade 2 building on the Government's list of places worth preserving. It has brick elevations partly whitened and a stylish tiled roof.

Inside, nobody has any excuse for not making a grand entrance when coming downstairs. The finest feature at Cowbeech is a William and Mary staircase in the entrance hall.

The skills of the 20th century have had their role to play as well. The property has been modernised and now the memory of William and Mary is kept warm by oil-fired central heating.

# Cowfold

One of the most noticeable houses in the Sussex village of Cowfold is the 700-year-old St Peter's Cottage, thought to have been a priest's house at one time.

Originally the timber framed building, with an infill of wattle and daub would have had timbers reaching the full height of the house, but over the years the lower beams have been replaced by brick.

The cottage, which is now a restaurant, displays the type of superior workmanship usually seen in churches in the area, with each mortice and tenon joint marked with Roman numerals. The present inglenook fireplace is a cast iron Sussex Fireback. It dates back to 1657.

# Cowfold

Not everyone's father can afford to give them a house on their wedding day, especially one as impressive as the Clock House, Cowfold.

In 1914 Mr James Rollshoare gave the house to his daughter, Muriel, on her marriage to Robin Loder whose family owns Leonardslee.

James Rollshoare had the 16th century house moved painstakingly from its original site further back from the road. At the same time various novel additions were made by architect Barry Parker.

He added two wooden wings to form the entrance court out of a halved barn found on the premises. The roof was made from Horsham stone an the original clock was put back on the ridge of the roof.

Captain Robin Loder was killed in World War One and his widow then moved to Leonardslee which her son, Sir Giles, now owns.

During World War Two the house was used by Canadian troops. While they were there, a fire destroyed the beautiful stone roof, the clock and the second floor.

The clock has never been replaced. When the second floor was restored, the roof was tiled. The Horsham stone couldn't be replaced either.

# Cross Bush

The tiny village of Cross Bush, near Arundel, is set in one of the most beautiful spots in Sussex. Yet it contains a community which seldom enjoys its attractions. For the 41 nuns of the Convent of Poor Clares at Cross Bush belong to a closed Order.

They came to Sussex in 1886 from Notting Hill, a not entirely tranquil area of London.

Although the nuns only have a limited knowledge of the countryside around them their community flourishes. Their number recently was made up by the transfer from Buckinghamshire of another community of nuns and the convent buildings now are being extended.

When the original nuns came from Notting Hill they moved into buildings designed by an architect called Headingham. His design was functional and tailored to meet the needs of the special residents. The red brick exterior merged harmoniously with the surrounding countryside.

Sussex is not entirely lost to the nuns. Occasionally they go to neighbouring Lyminster to visit the dentist or doctor — and to

exercise their democratic right to vote. But apart from that their Order specifies they must not leave the convent.

Inevitably the nuns and the people of Cross Bush seldom meet. However, it is certain the peace and beauty of the countryside outside is reflected within the walls of the convent of Poor Clares.

# Crowborough

Not a stone's throw from Baker Street — but miles from where Moriarty would ever dream of casting his scurrilous glances — there's a house in Sussex that, in world sleuth stakes, is the No. 1 shrine, or should we say exhibit.

Hush a little and you can almost hear Sherlock Holmes crack his boiled egg and turn the pages of The Times as he waits to set out and solve the next dastardly crime — from Windlesham Manor, near Crowborough.

To be more precise, it was a hut in the grounds where Sherlock used to be brought to life sipping port with Watson, while his creator Conan Doyle lived in the manor as a super author and writer of some of the biggest and best-selling books of all time.

From here Sherlock Holmes strolled forth to achieve crime-busting feats that the Flying Squad has never matched.

Creator Doyle had the house built himself in 1908 and also had much renovation work on the estate farm buildings carried out as well.

It was an ideal spot — near to London and yet enjoying the Sussex countryside and quietness which Doyle needed for his work.

It also gave the famous author the chance to indulge in his other passion — spiritualism.

Doyle did everything with more than style. He only moved from Windlesham Manor after he died here in 1936.

This man of words was originally buried beneath a tree in the manor grounds. But when the home he had lived in for many years was sold Doyle was exhumed, and his body found to be wrapped in a Persian carpet, so the story says.

He was reburied in a New Forest Church cemetery.

# Cuckfield

There was no doubting the eyes of Mr George Knott. They were definitely starry. But when he moved to the Tower House at Cuckfield he must have been over the moon.

It all happened last century and Mr Knott was, of course, an astronomer. This was eons before Jodrell Bank and in the heyday of that peculiar and declining phenomena, the Great British Amateur.

Mr Knott, in fact, reached the apex of acclaim and was mentioned as such in a footnote to the astronomy section in an Encyclopedia Britannica dated 1884.

The chapter came to fruition at Tower House, a mark II "stretched version" of a nearby house called Woodcraft, also still standing to this day.

Mr Knott had previously rented the property and during his stay grew to love it so much that he decided to have his temporary home copied with an exact replica.

He did, and Tower House rose in 1874 just a few doors away, together with everything identical, even down to cornice mouldings, but with an improved interior and benefiting from the addition of a splendid purpose-built observation tower.

It literally bristled with star-gazing equipment. One of the chief features was a transit room, a kind of viewing area on rails.

To the rails was fixed a high-powered, rock-steady telescope and the idea was that rather than scanning the heavens himself the gentleman astronomer sat back, watched and let the planets do the work by coming into his view as the night skies revolved.

Moveable equipment was housed at the top of the tower under the requisite dome, now replaced by a flat concrete roof.

# Ditchling

One of the most famous showplaces in Ditchling is the Anne of Cleves' House, which stands in the centre of the village.

The building is a near perfect example of Tudor architecture, although one resident has suggested the windows are more likely to be Elizabethan than original Tudor.

The house is supposed to have gained its name from the divorced wife of Henry VIII. The king gave Anne of Cleves the advowson — the right of presentation to a church benefice — of the church of Ditchling.

And with that went several manor houses in the area. This is one of them. But there is no evidence that suggests the lady herself ever lived there. Despite this, it stands out as a house of major importance in the village, and boasts an unusual outside staircase.

# Ditchling

Rowland Emett, O.B.E., creator of machines weird and wonderful, has a particularly apt phrase to describe his "early bird" habits.

He gets up each day at 5 a.m. and has finished half a day's work before some people even open their eyes.

"I'm the man who gets the larks up," he'll disarmingly tell you.

"It's a time when the world is quiet and peaceful. I feel perfect at that time of the day."

Mr Emett awakes in a cottage in the charming Sussex village of Ditchling.

It's called Wild Goose Cottage, an appropriate tag. It's not in fond remembrance of a feathered friend but of a flying Emett engine of the same name which was the centre of Emettania at the Festival of Britain.

Like most Emett productions the cottage is unlike anything else, a building that grew and went up around corners as its user's career grew.

Now it's a friendly, impromptu place where Mr Emett draws and plans his bizarre art work.

# Ditchling

The Old Meeting House, Ditchling, is thought to have been founded in 1698, and at the time was regarded as being very unorthodox.

It began as a place of worship for the General Baptist Assembly — a body of Baptists who believed in the authority of the scriptures, as interpreted by the individual.

The chapel was founded by Robert Chatfield of Streat in 1698, but records indicate that Matthew Caffyn of Horsham was one of the real leading lights in the movement.

In 1672, under the Declaration of Indulgence, two licences were issued for meetings in cottages in the village, and the Ditchling church sprang up from an amalgamation of all the little groups meeting in private houses.

Matthew Caffyn was expelled from Oxford for unorthodox beliefs, and was later called on to defend them before the General Baptist Assembly in about 1693. The Ditchling Congregation supported him loyally.

The church drew members from as far apart as Billinghurst, Lewes, Battle and Chailey, so Ditchling appears to have been the centre for Baptists in Sussex.

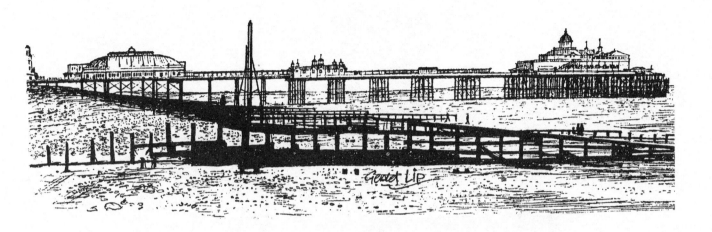

# Eastbourne

Those were the days — the Empire was at its height, Victoria ruled . . . and it only cost 2d to get on to Eastbourne Pier!

How times have changed. The Empire has gone, and the majority of piers, aided and abetted by rust and lack of cash, have followed.

Yet Eastbourne Pier proudly juts out to sea as a reminder of those once confident and expansive times.

It now shelters under the wing of big business. Its private enterprise protector is the giant Trust House Forte catering group, whose avowed intention is to maintain it as the finest in the land.

Work on the pier was begun in 1866. Four years later, on June 13, 1870, the pier was opened with all due pomp and circumstance by Lord Edward Cavendish, Duke of Devonshire.

In those days it was completely bare except for four kiosks at the gates and another four at the other end.

Lording over it all was the piermaster, aided by one boy and a toll-house keeper. Today more than 200 people work there.

The pier has taken the rough with the smooth. In 1875 and 1876 it suffered massive storm-damage.

In fact, the shore end was not just damaged — it simply wasn't there any more. Huge seas had washed it completely away.

But the sea wasn't allowed to win. The damaged section was replaced, but built on a higher level. It was joined to the rest of the structure by a slope — hence the distinctive shape of Eastbourne Pier.

In 1901 the theatre was opened. It went on to become the entertainment centre of Eastbourne. In 1903 the town's first film performance took place there.

Entertainment was presented 52 weeks a year until 1906 — even though the building remained without a therm of heating.

# Eastbourne

There are some rooms with views and some houses with views. But lighthouses always have views and there can be few to match Belle Tout.

This former house of light looks clear out over the English Channel at Eastbourne to the most splendid vista the South Coast has to offer.

Once though it sheltered the lighthouse men who kept shining the crucial oil light beacon for shipping.

Belle Tout — a Norman phrase meaning outlook — was built in 1834 and it wasn't until 1902 that progress snuffed out its light and it was replaced by the Beachy Head lighthouse.

Progress didn't make the structure redundant however and the 40 ft high tower and adjoining accommodation were soon converted into a house 400 feet above sea level which was home for a large part of the inter-war years to a London surgeon.

The war however wasn't so kind. Canadian troops were stationed on the Downs and whether by accident or spirited intention they managed to bomb the lighthouse and make a good job of it too — blowing off the roof.

It was down to a Mrs Cullinan, helped by her architect son, to put the damage right when she leased the property from Eastbourne Council in 1955, after it had been vacant during the intervening period.

The living accommodation was extended and the tower renovated with a bathroom on the ground floor, two bedrooms further up and a panoramic balcony on top of it all where the heart of the former lighthouse used to be.

# Eastbourne

A Birmingham man and an Eastbourne builder pooled their abilities almost 100 years ago to create the historic Eastbourne Town Hall.

Mr W. Foulkes was the Midlands architect and Mr James Peerless the local builder who had the task of transforming a plot of land into one of the town's most imposing buildings.

The site cost the authority £3,000; the building a further £35,000. It was opened by the mayor two years after the foundation stone was laid in 1886.

The building itself contains many links with history. Paintings of the town's mayors, the most famous one being perhaps Alderman Henry Keay, hung in the town hall. A woman has only once managed to gain a place in the gallery — in 1926 Miss Alice Hudson became mayor and held the office until 1928. And she managed to repeat the achievement again in 1943.

The mayor's parlour boasts a Victorian silver malice weighing 10¼lb., presented by Mr Carew Gilbert. The mayor's chain was presented by the Duke of Devonshire, and additional links to the chain have been added by subsequent mayors.

It can also boast the chain worn by the mayoress, the mayor's

ivory hammer, and assorted silver salvers and dishes and a silver ink stand — all presented by civic dignitaries over the years.

But one of the most ancient links with Eastbourne's past is the Constable's Tipstaff. Made of mahogany it is topped by a carved crown and also carries the Royal Arms, plus the words "Hundred of East Bourne".
feudal system of Domesday accounting.

It was presented in 1789, and was a sign of law and authority, carried by a sherrif's officer, bailiff or constable.

# Eastbourne

The Burlington Hotel, at Eastbourne, maybe Victorian, but the site itself offers insights into pre-history. The area on which the hotel is built is known to have been settled as far back as 1500 BC, and Bronze Age and Iron Age tools found on the site confirm this.

In Roman times Eastbourne became a settlement of some importance to the occupying forces. A large villa was built on the site of the hotel and its remains, including a Roman bath and portions of a corridor with tasselated pavement, have been unearthed. It is thought the villa was occupied by a Roman area commander or local governor.

The Eastbourne estate, on which the Burlington stands, was one of the several possessions of Saxon kings, including Alfred the Great and Edward the Confessor. But when William the Conqueror landed at nearby Pevensey he kept the Manor of Eastbourne for himself — and had it duly recorded as his in the Domesday Book, written 20 years later in 1086. Later still the estate passed to the Dukes of Devonshire, who still has close links with the town.

The Burlington was built during the mid-19th century and was

later one of the first hotels on the South Coast to offer guests artificially softened water, hot and cold running water and electric light. The hotel was designed to appeal to the Victorian aristocracy who were determined to enjoy the new pastime of sea bathing.

# East Grinstead

It looks peaceful now. But Old Stone House at East Grinstead must have possessed a different aura when Judge Jefferies, the notorious hang 'em all judge, used the premises as lodgings when an assize court was held here.

Those were the days of summary justice in the widest sense, when the stocks and gibbet stood in East Grinstead as a reminder of how direct was the judicial solution to trouble makers.

The assize has gone now leaving Old Stone House sitting in the town's Judges Terrace as a reminder of those days.

But there are other memories. The original building which stood here was put up in early medieval times by a guild of people called the Fraternity of Katherine, who in those distant centuries virtually ran the borough of East Grinstead and owned much property in the area.

By the early 16th century the building had become a pub, and some even say a bawdy house, known as The Sign of The George, the guild having been dissolved along with the monasteries by Henry VIII.

The property was rebuilt in the late 16th century and respectability came when the Crown emerged as the next owner, followed shortly afterwards by the Sackville family.

But they had to sell under the Reform Bill of 1832 and the Old Stone House then began a period of private doctors living in residence, which continued until it was bought by a property company, which turned it into the offices it is now.

The Old Stone House tag for the Jacobean building came, predictably enough, from the material used — Ardingly sandstone, called thus even though it was quarried in the East Grinstead area!

# Felpham

It's hard to think of poet, mystic and visionary William Blake having anything to do with the sleepy Sussex seaside resort of Felpham other than passing through it.

That he actually wrote such a lyrical verse about the place seems more than incredible viewed against Felpham of the 20th century:

Away to sweet Felpham for heaven is there:

The Ladder of Angels descends through the air

On the turret its spiral does softly descend.

Through the village it winds, at my cot does it end.

Modern Felpham has been swallowed up in the overspill development of Bognor and is bungalows, neat gardens and the middle-class trimmings that go with the hardly mystic atmosphere of a British retirement area.

But here William Blake did, indeed, for a time live, and the cottage, where he illustrated his prophetic book, Jerusalem, and began Milton, stands, plaque and all, in private occupation in the aptly-named Blake's Lane.

It was the poet and biographer William Hayley who brought

Blake down to Felpham for the four years he and his wife were to spend there.

The suggestion which brought him to Sussex at the age of 43, after seven productive years' work in Lambeth, was to engrave illustrations for a biography of Cowper.

In August, 1800, he first visited Felpham to rent Rose Cottage from the landlord of the nearby Fox Inn and he settled there the following month.

# Findon

The Domesday Book shows that there was a manor at Findon Place even in the time of Edward the Confessor.

It formed part of the huge estates in Sussex granted to William de Braose after the conquest.

He died at the house — which at that time was a hunting lodge with a 15,000 acre deer park.

Edward III stayed in the later stone-built manor house, built in the 13th century. Of this building two rooms have been identified and some foundations can be seen in the cellars.

Until the 16th century, Findon was owned by the Mowbray Earls of Norfolk. The manor then passed to Thomas Cromwell, Henry VIII's Lord Treasurer. Later, Richard Rich, Thomas More's betrayer took possession.

During the civil war the Royalist Earls of Thanet held Findon.

The future Charles II stayed at, or nearby, the manor while waiting to escape from this country via a boat from Shoreham.

The principal part of Findon Place was added to the nucleus of the original building by John Cheale, Norroy, King-at-Arms, in about 1740.

His grandson, William Green, still owned the property in 1780 when the music room was added for George, Prince of Wales, later the Prince Regent and George IV.

Extensive stables were built around 1800 by a later owner, William Richardson, a famous hunting squire. His coat-of-arms is carved above the entrance door.

Richardson's widow sold their pack of hounds to Lord Leconfield and they formed the stock of the present Leconfield Hunt.

The six bedroom Georgian manor house now stands in over nine acres, close to the A24.

# Firle Place

Firle Place, near Lewes, seat of Lord Gage is one of the few stately homes of Sussex that can claim to have been the home of the same family for centuries.

It was built in the mid-15th century during the reign of Henry IV and shortly afterwards bought by Sir John Gage.

In 1520 Sir John rebuilt and altered part of the original building, and part of his alterations still exist — the Tudor wing on the south of the building.

The Tudor wing ha a gable with moulded coping, and faced with Cean stone. The adjoining lower buildings date back to the early 18th Century. The roof is of Horsham slabs in contrast to the tiled roof the building had in Tudor times.

The projecting wing, with a hipped roof in the centre, was a companion gable of the Tudor front, but it has now been altered to bring it into line with the more modern work.

On the eastern end the mansion has a lofty screen front, incorporating the archway leading to a courtyard — once used for carriages.

The front is of French design, and simple but well proportioned. The modillion, cornice and pediment and the gateway arch with its Ionic pilasters all enhance the building's appearance.

# Fittleworth

When Louisa, widow of the first Duke of Abercorn, lived at Coates Castle, Fittleworth, in 1887, she found there was no railway station at the village.

Undeterred, she arranged for the London train to make an unscheduled stop there while she climbed aboard by standing on a chair brought for her by her footman.

She lived at Coates for 18 years until her death, aged 93, in 1905. During her stay she entertained countless children with lavish parties, including the young Winston Churchill.

The castle was built around 1810 in architect Horace Walpole's Strawberry Hill Gothic style. It is of stuccoed stone, and shaped like an inverted L, with crenelated gables and buttresses.

The house was built by John King, from Preston Candover, in Hampshire, and the doorway still bears his coat of arms — a lion rampant impaling the chevron between the three lions' heads of the Wyndhams.

He later married Charlotte, one of the six illegitimate children of the third Lord Egremont, and in 1858 sold the property to Charlotte's brother George, later created Baron Leconfield.

At the end of World War One, the Marquess of Hamilton lived at Coates with his five children, one of whom, Cynthia, became the Countess Spencer and grandmother of the present Princess of Wales.

At the time of Edward VII's funeral, the German Kaiser stayed at Coates and presented the Marquess with a gold bejewelled cigarette case.

In the 1920s this was found at the bottom of a well by an estate worker, possibly discarded at the outbreak of war.

During World War Two, Coates became the home of explosives enthusiast Col. Stewart Blacker, who converted the cellars to develop an anti-tank weapon.

# Glynde

If marks were handed out for original church building, Richard Trevor, Bishop of Durham, would be a top scorer. He was one of the Trevors of Glynde, the famous family which for centuries has been connected with the Glynde Place stately home in this quiet Sussex village.

Trevor was a favourite of George II at the London court. When he wasn't too busy doing the work of the Lord in the north, he spent much time expanding the Sussex family home, where he lived from 1707 until 1771.

An additional achievement of his was the building of Glynde Church, an Italianate-looking building in pure Renaissance style, unlike any other in the county and probably the country.

This fashionable-looking building was paid for by the bishop largely from his own pocket.

The architect was one Thomas Robinson and he sat down at his drawing board directly after returning from a trip to Florence.

He came back with the customary English obsession with things classical, so its Italian good looks are not really surprising.

The church was only finished in 1765. But it has much about it that is visually fascinating, even if it has come in for the odd sniping from the architectural purists.

It was built by the firm of John Morris of Lewes, in Portland stone. Over its porch it has the shield of arms of Bishop Trevor and the see of Durham.

Inside there's a fine and notable plaster ceiling and fabric-covered walls.

Chancel windows are unusual, too, because they contain panels of 16th century Flemish glass scriptural scenes.

They were erected in honour of Viscount Hampden, speaker of the house of Commons, who also lived at Glynde House and who died in 1892.

# Goodwood

Goodwood House has had a history chequered with colourful owners. It's been visited by the Royal Family who enjoy Goodwood Races.

The house was built in 1660 — the core is still intact — and remained a small country house until 1697.

Charles, First Duke of Richmond, was the son of King Charles II and Louise Kerouaille, a French spy in the employ of Louis XIV.

When King Charles died Louise and her son were shipped back across the Channel. Son Charles stole her jewels and ran away to England. He was a hunting fanatic and bought Goodwood House as a lodge.

The Second and Third Dukes of Richmond were great patrons of the arts. The second Duke gave Italian artist Cannelletto his first commission when he arrived in England.

The third Duke increased the estates from 1,100 to 17,000 acres, and enlarged the house twice.

In 1760, he commissioned architect Sir William Chambers to build the house into a substantial H-shape.

The fifth and sixth dukes mortgaged all the estates to build better houses for their tenants, to provide water for the cottages and keep down the rents.

The estates were therefore in hock when the seventh and eighth Dukes inherited. Since 1930, 3,000 acres of beech forest have been sold to help pay off the mortgage and all Scottish properties were auctioned off.

Frederick Charles, ninth Duke of Richmond is in his seventies and the estate is run by a group of companies of which his eldest son Lord March is chairman.

'THRAVES'. GRAFFHAM.

# Graffham

It may seem a rash deed in retrospect, but when the steward of a large country estate at Graffham tore up and burned the deeds to homes there he did it for a reason — to stop them falling into the hands of Germans, then poised to invade Sussex and England during the First World War.

The threat passed — the deeds and some historical records with them, unfortunately — but Graffham remained as a prime example of an English village.

Certainly the church had seen history, dating back as it does to at least the Domesday period. Two great churchmen are associated with Graffham, Bishop Samuel Wilberforce, son of the slavery-fighting William, and Cardinal Manning.

The cardinal certainly sent ecclesiastical eyebrows soaring.

He was a curate in Graffham and married the daughter of his rector in 1833.

He eventually became rector and was appointed archdeacon of Chichester — but ten years later became a Roman Catholic convert. Despite the scandal he became Roman Catholic archbishop of Westminster within 14 years and a cardinal by 1875.

Earlier residents probably weren't so settled. In Celtic times people in this area probably lived on the Downs and descended into the forest for game.

There are five Bronze Age barrows on Graffham Down and evidence of Saxon occupation.

By Norman times there is evidence of Graffham men testifying to how much land the village owned — about 1,200 arable acres supporting a population of about 100.

# Greatham

Hope springs eternal, they say — and so does water from the ground around Quell Farm at Greatham. This delightful corner of Sussex near Pulborough is blessed with myriad delights at ground level and bubbling springs below.

When farmer Mr. Rivers Batchelor and his wife turn on the taps the water comes from their own reservoir, which is topped up from four of seven springs.

What's more, the water sparkles and tastes like nectar, say those lucky enough to sip it. Some years ago the water authority descended from on high to see if the spring's production was clean and suitably sterile to drink.

This DIY supply of water goes back deep into history. The Batchelors were visited by some Austrian friends some years ago, and they pointed out that quell is a German word meaning "source of the spring."

So that could explain the farm's strange name if not how such a Germanic label ended up in deepest Sussex.

The farm itself is at least 500 years old, as its sturdy oak beams prove. Once it was almost certainly a yeoman's cottage, and today it is still the centre of a large mixed agricultural operation of dairy and arable farming.

The Batchelor's time at the farm goes back to 1899 when a family forerunner came up from Cornwall and bought the land for what in those days must have the more than tidy sum of £21,000. Some of that original estate has been sold since, but a large slice remains.

Naturally there is a ghost. No one is too sure what his identity is but people will tell you they feel a "presence." It's friendly though, and no bother.

But Greatham has the effect of making people feel more alive. Alice Maynell, the poet, wrote there until her death in 1922.

For her, this part of Sussex proved the inspiration it still is for those lucky enough to call it home.

PENNS ROCKS GROOMBRIDGE

# Groombridge

It's a long way from Sussex to Pennsylvania. But thumb back through the pages of history and you'll find links that bring them closer together.

Pennsylvania was founded by the great Quaker, William Penn. He fits into the Sussex historical picture by virtue of having taken his wife from Sussex and having owned the superb house that bears his name in the hamlet of Withyham, on the north west fringes of the Ashdown Forest and up near the county border.

The house is called Penn's in the Rocks, a double-barrelled title that hints at more of the story lying behind it. The rocks referred to are the outcrops that abound in the area of Tunbridge Wells sandstone, and in this particular case one massive outcrop that juts from the green countryside just above the house.

Thousands of years ago they provided shelter and cover for Penn's forerunners here. Visitors came in Mesolithic and Neolithic times and pottery found in the recesses of the rocks has been dated at between 3000 to 2000 B.C.

Penn's rock itself was owned by the Penn family for 90 years, from 1672 to 1762. In those days it was called Rocks Farm and as such is passed from William Penn down to his son, grandson and great-grandson.

BROOMHAM

# Guestling

Headmaster Claude Rackett had heard all the ghost stories about spectral fingers switching on lights in Broomham School at Guestling, near Hastings.

Locals linked them with rumours of a lady in blue who walked at first-floor level outside the 16th century building. It all plainly needed some homework by way of investigation. So Mr. Rackett strode forth.

He paced at night outside the premises, looked up — and saw the lights. They followed him as he strode along, seeming to be switched on and off in rooms to keep pace.

But it wasn't a ghost. It wasn't even a spirited wayward lad trying new psycho-shock tactics against luckless teachers.

The lights were eerie reflections from street lamps two miles away and the rest was a reflection on fertile imaginations. So, too, was the blue lady. Mr Rackett has never seen her.

All the same, Broomham is the kind of place that should have spirit boarders as well as the boys at this coaching prep school.

It was built for the Ashburnham family in the 16th century. The site was reputed to have been occupied by a lady called Edydd back in the ninth century, although Mr. Rackett can find nothing in the Sussex county archives to support this.

At that time it was called Brunham and it continued down the years until 1925 when the present building was completely refurbished and reduced in size over a two-year period.

# Hailsham

History has its roots firmly in the ground at Windmill Hill Place, near Hailsham. This graceful house stands seven miles from the sea, overlooking Herstmonceux Castle and with splendid downland views.

Its gardens are a horticultural must — their particularly sheltered and mild grounds open in the spring. Flourishing still is a venerable cork tree that is a direct link with the Peninsular War and Napoleonic days.

A son of the family who lived at Windmill Hill Place fought in the British Army of the day. When he came back he brought in his pocket several cork acorns from woods where the trees flourished.

They were duly planted and one still lives on, together with many other rare plants and shrubs. It doesn't stop at cork. There are the Waterloo Chestnuts as well, similarly brought back as seeds from the famous battlefield.

Windmill Hill Place itself dates back through the centuries, with ancient maps always showing a dwelling of some sort here.

It gained the name because of two windmills situated on adjoining hills, one of which has withstood the ravages of time.

The present house was built for Mr. William Pigeon and finished in 1798.

# Handcross

Sympathy, please, for owners of houses that win the Derby. After you have banked the winnings, drunk the champers and fixed the stud fee how does one provide a lasting memorial to the occasion? One man who wrestled with the problem was the redoubtable Col. G. H. Loder, whose mount Spion Kop cantered first past the post to win back in the genteel year of 1920.

The colonel was a member of the family who created the greatly gardens of Leonardslee and Wakehurst, and he lived in the splendours of High Beeches at Handcross.

It was here that Spion Kop had his memorial oats — by way of this suitably impressive tower that Col. Loder had built specially on the old coach house. The clock was added for another lucky day at the races with another winner in 1928.

Tributes to memory, it seems, are made of lasting stuff. During the last war the old High Beeches was the victim of an enemy plane direct hit and was thus destroyed.

Only Spion Kop's clock tower survived the blitz and now the old building lives usefully on as accommodation for farm equipment.

# Hartfield

Acting as custodians to the memories of Winnie the Pooh and dead Rolling Stone Brian Jones is a full-time job. So much so that the family now living in the Hartfield House are happy to keep a low profile.

But Cotchford Farm as the home in question certainly doesn't. Each year it attracts dozens of visitors. Largely they are Americans drawn to this Sussex retreat by the Pooh myths of childhood that today's young still find appealing.

They come by car and by coachload to savour this 15th century six-bedroom farm standing in two acres of formal gardens and in as perfect a country setting as one would expect.

Some are so bold and curious that they knock at the door and insist they see the room now used as a playroom where A. A. Milne used to write during his years here from 1929 to 1959.

They see where Christopher Robin was breathed into imaginative life and said his first prayers, and look at the actual famous Pooh tree with a hole in it in the back garden.

When Winnie was 50 years old, scores of top publishing executives tramped down to the old Sussex stamping grounds again to wish the Pooh a happy birthday in his old home.

Others with a different, less healthy approach to life have a lingering morbid curiosity about Brian Jones. He died in the swimming pool here after owning the house for a short time.

Again, it is the Americans who are in the forefront of this retrospective interest.

Recently a letter arrived at Hartfield asking for pictures of the pool and all the information. It was understandably left unanswered.

The Cotchford Farm family say they would need a professional secretary to do justice and deal with everyone wanting to know about the place and its background.

They do show the occasional visitor around, but prefer to play hosts to their own privacy.

And after all, avid readers of Pooh know where his proper home is — between the pages of those magic books.

# Henfield

The 500-year-old Mockbridge House, in Henfield, stands as a tribute to the courage of a remarkable Sussex authoress. The modest book, The Roadmender, appeared to delight its readers — and confound the critics — with no story or narrative, relating commonplace events within distance of "the little church at the foot of the grey green down" or "the field of daffodils".

The true story of The Roadmender was only revealed after its author died. Its first chapter appeared in a magazine in the name of Michael Fairless, it was then serialised and republished and many asked who was Mr. Fairless.

The answer must have come as quite a shock — because "he" was none other than a former nurse, Margaret Fairless Barber, a woman of extraordinary courage and determination.

All the time she wrote she lay paralysed, with her writing pad propped up on her chest. From her bed she could see Mock Bridge, which crossed the River Adur by the main road, the old mill and the nearby Bull Inn.

Her story came from memories of her life as a district nurse, the local people, the tramps and unskilled labourers.

As she weakened she lost the use of her right hand, and so learned to write with her left — all the time delighting her readers who were unaware of the struggle behind the words. She spent the last two years of her life writing the book and was buried in the Sussex churchyard at Ashurst, near Steyning. She was just 33.

# Henfield

Traces of St. Giles Church, Henfield, which was recorded in the Domesday Book, are still visible. However, most of the present church, which stands on the site of a Saxon church, was built in the Middle Ages.

Much of the work was done between 1677 and 1706, and the beams used to "tie-in" the church walls were old ship's timbers installed in 1710.

St. Giles has a 13th century octagonal sandstone font and a wooden shingle spire with two bells. It seats about 80 people.

The church has box pews with doors dating from the 18th century, with the names of all the houses in the parish carved on the sides.

Each house had two pews in the church — a comfortable one at the front for the family and a harder one at the back for the servants.

Two of the church windows depict the story of St. Giles. One shows him defending a deer shot and wounded by a hunting party.

The church is in an isolated position in relation to Henfield village, and this is attributed to the Black Death.

It is believed the village, which was originally built around the church, was wiped out when the plague struck, leaving only the church standing.

When people returned to the area they preferred to build down near the river with its bridge rather than on the hill near the church.

Lists of vicars of St. Giles go back to the 14th century.

# Henfield

Woods Mill, near Henfield, the headquarters of the Sussex Trust for Nature Conservation, is a bastion of the countryside, determinedly resisting the ever advancing tide of concrete and development.

Ramshorn snails, mayfly nymph and the Town Hall Clock plant, with its tiny fragrant flowers are all to be found on the nature reserve by the mill. And on the stonework of the mill itself Hart's Tongue Fern flourishes, with its strap shaped leaves bearing rust coloured spores on the underside during summer.

It was in 1966 that a private donor came to the rescue of a group of naturalists who badly needed a new headquarters — and knew exactly what they wanted. An 18th century house, water mill, lake and 15 acres of land fitted the bill exactly and the naturalists had their base.

There has been a water mill on the site since at least 1374 — and possibly for much longer, as they were used widely in Britain from the 9th century. The present mill dates from the 18th century, and the present wheel and machinery were installed in the 1850s during a complete overhaul.

The mill now has a turning water wheel and houses a new wildlife and countryside exhibition which includes a 25 foot high model of an oak tree.

The earliest sale notice on the mill dates from 1770. It was then described as a freehold estate comprising a water corn

mill, with three pairs of stones, two bolting mills and two water wheels.

Miller John Botting had the longest stay: 30 years, from 1828 to 1858. He was followed by George Holman who stayed until 1878, and the last to work the mill was Caleb John Coote who took over in 1916 and stayed until 1927.

Sussex millwright Mr. P. Stenning also played a big part in the mill's varied history, by industriously recovering millstones from the grounds and re-building part of the machinery.

# Horsham

Christ's Hospital school was founded in 1552 in London in an attempt to deal with the problems posed by increasing numbers of sick and poor in the city. Over the years it became a prestigious educational centre, sending its first pupils to Oxford and Cambridge in the 1560's.

In 1877 a Royal Commission decided the time had come for the school to be moved from London. In spite of protests from the Duke of Cambridge the whole school moved to Horsham on May 29, 1902. The 1,200 acres bought from the Aylesbury Dairy for Christ's Hospital cost just £47,000, while the entire bill for the building came to £546,000.

The architects, Sir Aston Webb and Ingress Bell managed to embody some of the features of the London building into their Horsham plans, such as the Wren Arch, the Grecian's Arch, the Old Science School and the Chapel. The school also boasts one of the largest quadrangles in the country, at the centre of which stands a fountain surmounted by a leaden statue of Edward VI. But not everyone was pleased with the school buildings, and some contemporary critics described it as an "arrogant brick town."

# Horsham

Knepp Castle may have its roots in a proud and colourful past, but its damp nose also points to the future as well — in the gentle shape of cows.

The Knepp herd of pedigree Danish Reds is famous throughout the world, which on the one hand sends visitors to this corner of Sussex near Horsham to see how it's done and on the other receives the cattle as valued exports.

Sir Walter Burrel, present lord of the manor and farmer of renown, can trace his family history here for misty centuries.

Knepp Castle No. 1 goes all the way back to King John, who often stayed to hunt in the area.

His steward here in those days was one Roland Bloet and in 1213 he wrote to him: "We send you our huntsman with ten lads and five keepers and ten horses and 114 dogs and five greyhounds to hunt for deer in the park at Knepp and we command you to find them in reasonable expenses as long as they shall be with you, for which it shall be computed to you at the Exchequer."

Destroy rather than hunt was the directive just three years later though. King John wanted Knepp knocked down to keep it from the hands of King Louis of France who at the time was threatening Southern England with invasion.

So down the castle eventually came, although you have a choice of precisely when. Sir William Waller, besieger of Chichester and Bramber during the Civil War in 1642, is credited with the dark deed.

Then again there's another demolition date of 1762 when it is reputed to have been knocked down for Sussex road building material.

Knepp Castle No. 2 was built not far away for £19,000 in 1809.

# Horsted Keynes

Ludwell Grange, built in 1540, is one of the oldest homes in Horsted Keynes.

Like so many romantic country homes it was originally a working farm.

The roof was built of Horsham stone and the outside walls hung with Sussex tiles.

But 50 years ago the Grange was modernised and extended — though still using old-fashioned materials so that it retained its rustic charm.

Tiles were replaced with plaster and timbers and the house has five bedrooms now where before it had three.

The interior boasts some of the most interesting features with attractive panelling, dating back to the 16th century, in the sitting room.

There panels, like the ceiling beams, have Roman numerals cut into them. This shows that they were probably constructed elsewhere before being used at Ludwell Grange.

The present owner says that the house — with its distinctive chimneys — was once an inn.

Exactly when is uncertain — though it was probably around the early 1900s.

# Horsted Keynes

The Old House at Birch Grove, Horsted Keynes earns the "Old" in its name by going back to at least the first part of the 17th century. It was built by Sir Richard Michelbourne, who died in 1638 and who is buried in Horsted Keynes church.

Sir Richard owned a lot of land and the administration of such a hefty chunk of real estate was obviously a full-time task.

The chap to whom this duty fell was known as a reeve. The perk of the job in this case was The Old House, which in those days was known as The Reeve's House.

By the time of William Michelbourne, the property' true value appears to have been realised, and he wrote to an occupier in the middle of the 17th century as a social equal.

Historians have deduced from the clue that a kinsman had moved in and shifted the house well and truly up-market.

Today the Government shares that enthusiasm and the property is on the official list of heritage buildings constituting architectural and historical interest.

Horsted Keynes has not been a backwater place in the history of Sussex. The village is famous for the Rev. Giles Moore, the rector from 1656 to 1680, who kept a day-book which is now known to social historians throughout the country.

In the pages of this early diary, the minister jotted down minute observations of life in those times, making it one of the most faithful pictures of rural life in the 17th century we have.

# Houghton

You could say that the farming Ayling family is well established at Houghton, deep in West Sussex near Arundel.

Time is measured more slowly in the countryside and when you have a farming ancestor named John Ayling in the local churchyard with an 1830 date his tombstone, you are entitled to feel like sons of the local soil.

It has been from Old Farm at Houghton that the family has carried on its time — honoured traditions.

The farmhouse is about as traditional Sussex as it is possible to find. The roof is thatched in straw, it has daub and wattle walls, with ship's timbers for beams. The date is at least early 15th century and possibly much earlier.

It seems likely that farmers have been the occupants down the ages, leading right to the present day, with Mr William Ayling and his son.

Earlier members of the Ayling family cooked on traditional spits, and at one time the flagstone floor was covered in sand, which was swept out and thrown on to the garden once a week.

Everthing was much closer to the earth than in these modern times. Water, for instance, had to be hauled up from a deep well in the garden, topped with a concrete lid some years ago to stop investigative children.

Today the farm, still part of the Norfolk estate, has changed from being mixed arable and dairy to being solely dairy, with a growing herd of Friesians to meet the demands of high intensity farming.

# Houghton

It's no exaggeration to say that Houghton House, on the borders of Arundel Park, is as pretty as a picture. Arthur Rackham, described by many as the greatest book illustrator ever, lived here so you'd expect him to have an eye for architectural beauty.

The house and the 15 acres that surrounded it were the palette board of serenity which helped Rackham conjure forth so many entrancing pictures, the most famous of them for children's books.

Grimm's Fairy Tales, Alice in Wonderland and Wind in the Willows all blossomed into illustrative life from the hand of this genius.

For 12 years this serene Sussex retreat was home for Rackham, who fished in the nearby Arun. Eventually he moved back to London and died in 1939. The artist left plenty of marks on the house itself, souvenirs of the nicest kind.

He was wont to carve little sculptures as reminders of his presence on the doors such as fleur-de-lis, which are still at Houghton House now.

He designed tiles, too, and his wife came in on the creative act by planning the garden layout.

The house itself has its own claim to fame in addition to that of its best-known occupant — notably its age and style.

It is thought to be about 400 years old and is built in Georgian and Tudor styles. The deeds to right back to the reign of Charles I.

# Hove

Hove's Brunswick Square is one of the best examples of Regency terraced architecture in the country and follows closely the lines of the terraces in London's Regent's Park.

Brunswick Terrace and Brunswick Square were both built between 1825 and 1827 and are similar to earlier terraces in Kemp Town.

They were financed by the Rev. Thomas Street who owned the Wick Estate in Brighton. The architects were A. Wilds and Busby.

Each of the terraces has 39 bays and the square, thought not as large as Lewes Crescent and Sussex Square, is certainly grandiose enough to be a local landmark.

Both the ranges of Brunswick Terrace have three storeys and a centre of ten giant columns. Above the top storey is an attic, instead of a pediment as in Sussex Square.

Brunswick Terrace was pulled back from the brink two years ago by a banking corporation after it fell into disrepair. They bought the property to convert into flats and sold off part for a hotel.

The corporation had to completely rebuild the inside of the Regency shell and replace the roof.

Most of the decay set in after a developer bought the terrace and then went broke.

But the importance of the property was highlighted by the government which gave a grant of £50,000 towards part of the restoration, an unusually large sum to part with for one terrace.

# Hove

The Hove Museum of Art was built between 1873 and 1876, and is housed in Brooker Hall in Hove. The first owner was John Vallance, who became lord of the manor in 1867, and his widow continued to live in the house until 1913.

During World War One the building housed German prisoners, and people used to gather round the walls to peer inside.

After the war the house lay empty until 1926. Hove Corpora-tion then bought it as a museum, and the rooms were laid out to represent furnishings in Sussex during different periods.

They included a Georgian, Regency and Victorian rooms and a Sussex farm kitchen. In the grounds, to the east of the building, lies the Jaipur Gateway, presented to the town by the Imperial Institute when the museum first opened and originally built for the Maharajah of Jaipur.

The teak used in the gateway was cut in Bombay and sent to Jaipur to be carved by the Maharajahs' subjects.

# Hove

Private Schools in Brighton and Hove were famous and prolific towards the end of the last century.

But perhaps the most famous gained its fame from one of its pupils, Winston Churchill, who went to the Misses Thompson's Preparatory School at Lansworth House in Brunswick Road, Hove.

There is a commemorative plaque on the house to show this, and it gives the dates of his stay as 1883, 1884 and 1885.

Churchill then went on to study at Harrow, but while at the school wrote to his father about his experiences there. .

In one letter, he wrote: "At this school I was allowed to read things which interested me: French, history, lots of poetry by heart and above all riding and swimming. The impression of those years makes a pleasant picture in my mind, in strong contrast to my earlier schoolday memories."

One of the reasons for choosing the school, besides the advantage of the sea air, was that it was near the family doctor, Robson Roose. It was just as well, because in 1886 young Winston nearly died from pneumonia.

On March 15, 1886, Dr Roose wrote to Lord Randolph: "We are still fighting the battle for your boy. His temperature is 103 now, but he is taking his nourishment better and there is no increase of lung mischief."

# Hurstpierpoint

It's nice to live in an old house of character. It's even better to live in an Elizabethan one with years of ancestral history behind it.

Such is Danny House, the Elizabethan mansion lying in acres of green Sussex at Danny Park, Hurstpierpoint.

Today it is home for residents in a housing association for people who have spent their lives in public service. Once it was the home of the Campion family.

It was in 1502 that the building of Danny started and the Campions came on the scene in 1702.

The oldest part of the mansion is the north wing and middle block, both built in the early years of the 16th century.

In 1593 Charles Goring reconstructed and enlarged the buildings into an E-shaped plan, with the open side facing east.

This side, with its stone mullioned windows looking out now on a modern world of technology, still largely retains its original appearance despite being renewed in places.

The south side had a new front grafted on to it one hundred years later by Henry Campion and Barbara Courthope and much of the charm of Danny today comes from a blend of Tudor and 18th century architectural styles.

Inside you'll find 16th and 17th century panelling looking as good as new.

Also in pristine condition is a chimney piece with the date proudly stamped on it of 1571 and a timber horseshoe-shaped staircase which was part of alterations made in 1728.

The Campions are not far away either, in person or artisitc presence.

There is a collection of their family portraits hanging here, including one of Sir William Campion, whose armour stands in the hall.

His metal suit didn't save him — he was killed at the siege of Colchester in 1684.

# Hurstpierpoint

Look through the residents list of Pakyns Manor down the ages and you'll find a historical Who's Who guide to some of the most important and well-placed families in yesteryear Sussex.

It's not every house that can trace its history back to 1157 and a list of occupants is invariably that much harder to come by.

But at this Hurstpierpoint house we can still peep at a rollcall of its ancient householders.

The property is said to take its name from Paganus, who was Sheriff of Sussex. Paganus is though to have been connected with the Pierpoints who were the early possessors of the manor of Hurst.

Anyway it was the Pakyns family who first settled here, ranging from Walter in 1216 to William de Pakyn in 1292 and Simon Pakyn in 1304.

The line of possession went right on down to William Pakyn in 1491 and probably the last member of the family to hold the manor was one Roger Pakyn in 1509.

Hot on the heels of these first owners came John Burtenshaw in 1535, but good fortune didn't bless this latest family. John Burtenshaw junior was found guilty of murder and felony and by 1547 the manor and lands in Hurstpierpoint had come into the ownership of a Richard Holden.

The following years throw up a host of families and people who must have enjoyed living in this fine Susssex house — the Luxfords, the Fynes, the Threels, the Shorts, the Scrases, the Butchers and not least to the Borrers.

Their occupancy was one of the most distinguished. William Borrer bought the manor while living at the now vanished Bishopshurst, a large house at Albourne.

His son, another William who lived from 1753 to 1832, was the High Sheriff for Sussex and raised a troop of horse for the country's defence against Napoleon.

His son was yet another William Borrer, this time the distinguished botanist whose name still rings a bell in the present day.

# Hurstpierpoint

You can't help almost a laugh of relief when you hear that the thirteenth century has beaten the technological twentieth. One such tiny encounter was acted out and won handsomely by yesterday's team at Pigwidgeon Cottage, at leafy Hurstpierpoint.

It featured a handful of impassive, centuries-old oaken beams versus Today's confident central heating installation men, armed with heavy masonry drills and a warning from the cottage owner that they were in for a hard time.

The result? Five steel-hardened drills snapped clean off, head scratching by installation men and a respectful truce before efforts started again.

Obviously perseverence finally won through, but not before Pigwidgeon Cottage had proved a hardiness that stretches all the way back to 1460.

For a start, nails can't go rusty here, mainly because there aren't any. The whole show is held together by a series of wooden pegs, still tight and snug in their timber sockets today.

Once, too, the cottage was thatched and before the "modern" improvement of thatch came along it had an elemental kind of woven wood roof, filled in with moss and dirt for that final insulating touch.

Inside is pretty unusual also, thanks, in part, to a dragon beam ceiling of extremely rare design in the dining room, a bread oven still existing in the inglenook fireplace and walls three feet thick in places and strengthened by daub and wattle.

The minstrels gallery would give performers a few headaches if they returned to entertain from it today though.

A floor has been fitted to divide the previous open space into two rooms, so the players would be looking down and playing to a set of floor boards that in turn are a downstairs ceiling.

# Hurstpierpoint

In a village overflowing with interesting buildings, one of the most unusual is the Tower at Hurstpierpoint.

It was built in 1827 by the Weeks Family, who also owned nearby Mansion House.

It was probably built as a watchtower to spy on visitors to the village coming from the direction of the New Inn, a building that still stands today.

It was probably built as a watchtower to spy on visitors to the village coming from the direction of the New Inn, a building that still stands today.

It is also possible that the tower was built as a folly, an idea popularised by the Victorians, but also present in Georgian architecture.

A folly served no useful purpose. It was merely an exhibition of the owner's sense of fun, or ability to pay for the building.

Later, the Tower became a smokers' retreat, the only place the man of the house was allowed to enjoy a quiet pipe or cigar.

Other buildings of interest in the village include the theatre, which is equipped with an ornate Edwardian pediment above the entrance, and detailing reminiscent of an Indian temple.

Also important is Pakyns Manor, which can trace its history back to 1157.

# Hurstpierpoint

Intrigued passers-by often stop to take a good long look at Randolphs Farm near Hurstpierpoint.

Set in 260 acres of Sussex farmland, the house has several striking and imposing Elizabethan chimney stacks. The stacks are built in the same mellow-red patterned brickwork as the rest of the farmhouse.

Estimates vary as to when Randophs Farm was originally built, and there is no firm evidence. The present occupier, Mr Randolph Jenkin, says that the building has been dated back to the early 1600s, adding: "It could well go back even before that, unfortunately there is no way of tracing any more records."

The farmhouse started life as a two up, two down house. The existing oak beams and inglenook fireplace that formed the core are still intact. Over the years the house has been added to and the original front of the building now forms the back. Randolphs Farm is part of the Danny estate, and is situated half-way between Hurstpierpoint and Wolstanbury Hill.

# Keymer

If you visit one particular mill in Sussex this summer, you'll probably find it's a bit down at heel.

But not for long. The building in question is the mill at Keymer, at present a degree or two ground down by the passage of time. Right now what it has in memories it lacks in sails, because two of them blew off in a particular vigorous winter storm.

Yet like all good stories, the mill is about to take a turn for the better. The Hassocks Amenity Association, with the full blessing of the mill's owners, the Sussex Archaeological Society, is about to wave a restoration wand and put the old girl back on her feet.

She will probably never be put back into working order, but to the tourist's eye the mill will once again look a "live" part of the scenic tapestry.

There was a mill on this spot in Keymer back in Domesday times, and the current example is probably about 200 years old, possible older.

It is of the post mill type, so called because the whole affair used to revolve on a stout oak post to catch any favourable turns of the breeze.

A siting at the junction of three very old tracks meant that Keymer Mill was a very important centre in the agricultural life of this part of Sussex. It kept on working right up to the First World War.

But, like all things, progress and mechanisation took their toll. Steam and electric mills were quicker and cheaper, and the mill at Keymer fell into disrepair. Eventually time ate away much of the fabric and the innards too. So what you see today is a little more than a shell.

Luckily, this is one special shell that still has a more than useful life ahead.

# Keymer

A name that catches the imagination — and an equally colourful history — belong to St. Cosmas and St. Damian church in Keymer.

Cosmas and Damian, medical missionaries from Syria, who were martyred in the 4th century, are that church's patron saints.

Keymer's church is one of only five in the country to have this special dedication.

The history of the church goes back at least to the time of the Norman Conquest in 1066. Some surviving parts are possibly Saxon.

The Domesday Book of 1086 records a church at "Chemer," and from then until 1536 the Keymer Church, and those at Clayton, were served by priests sent from the St. Pancras Priory at Lewes.

Records beyond that date remain uncertain, but it is known that from 1752 the priests were sent from Brasenose College, Oxford.

In one of the windows of the north aisle, the arms of the college can still be seen.

Most of the building standing today was built after 1866, the date the church was re-built. Before then the church consisted of the chancel, nave, tower and south porch.

The nave and tower were demolished and re-built with the architect, E. E. Scott, retaining the 14th century style in the new building.

The apsidal chancel was restored, but a possibly pre-1066 chancel arch and a window were retained.

A south aisle was also added and during the work the foundations of an earlier one were found.

This provided another piece of evidence for the likelihood of a late Saxon church existing on the site.

# Lancing

What's in a name? A whole host of different names is attached to the Old Posting House at North Lancing.

Once it was Walnut Tree Cottage and another tenant thought it would be nice to call it Grants Farm House.

The property probably has had its present colourful label for only about 50 years.

But its past stretches into dim history. There was a house on the site well before the present one, and today's occupants, Dr. George Shaw and his wife, have a formidable list of residents dating back to 1200.

Today's Old Posting House is hardly a junior. It dates back to around 1540.

Dr. Shaw, a biologist who is head of the science department at nearby Lancing College, still wonders about the reson for a mysterious underground passage which leads from the house.

The bricked-up remains can be seen in the basement and one possible reason for its use was as a smugglers' getaway.

The house has five bedrooms set cosily under a Horsham slab roof. It is listed by the Government as a building of historic interest.

The Shaws have been here for only three years but they have lived in Lancing for 20 and often in the past cast the keenest of eyes on the building, which is regularly illustrated on postcards.

There are many visitors, particularly Americans at the height of the tourist season. Local schoolchildren often drop in for lessons on how their forerunners used to live.

At the Old Posting House they see a timber-framed building, with an 18th century brick front, abounding.

# Lewes

One of the most picturesque parts of Lewes is Keere Street. Cobbled surfaces and houses of flint and mellowed brick hug the course of the old town wall.

Keere Street, often call ed the stiffest walk in town, can be traced back more than 700 years unchanged. It appears as "the path called Kerestreete" in a deed dated 1272.

Legend has it that George IV, when Prince of Wales, drove a coach and four down its steep incline for a wager. It is now closed to traffic.

The fine half timbered 15th century bookshop at the top of the street indicates what many Lewes houses must have been like before receiving their Georgian facades.

The bookshop has a history dating it back to 1450, and a list of tenants stretching as far back as 1750. In that year records show the building housed a firm of clay pipe manufacturers.

At the bottom of Keere Street is a fine vantage point from which to view the town walls stretching eastwards and northwards.

# Lewes

William Laird could aptly be called the architect of his own misfortune. He bought Southover Grange, Lewes, in 1871 from a Captain Wyndham and promptly decided the building could be improved upon.

Laird managed to change an attractive Elizabethan building into what was then the Victorian vogue. But he decided he didn't like the changes and never lived there.

The house was originally built in 1572 by William Newton using stones from Lewes Priory. It was then known as Southover House.

Later, in 1630, William Newton's second son married Jane Stansfield, the maternal grandmother of diarist John Evelyn, who lived there until 1637 while he was going to the nearby grammar school.

And Southover Grange has other famous names linked with it. In the 1790s the Prince of Wales, later the Prince Regent and King George IV, often stayed there.

# Lewes

St. Michael's Church, Lewes, is thought to have been built originally to serve the town's castle in the 13th century.

Its pebbledash spire rises from an unusual Norman round flint tower, of which there are only three in Sussex.

The southern arcade of the three bays dates from the 14th century, but the east bays to the chapel were built several hundred years later in 1748.

The street front is from the same date, but the windows are classically Gothic and were built in 1885. The two doorways with roundels are Georgian.

It boasts 1880s stained glass in the south chapel and south aisle, which is probably by Powells.

The church's interesting brasses include an early 15th century brass to a knight, which was originally 3ft. long but is now headless.

95

# Lindfield

Making Henry VIII laugh can't always have been easy — but it seems to have been profitable. Paxhill Park, Lindfield, was built for his court jester's son Ninian Boord between 1595 and 1606. It's a 60-room Grade Two Elizabethan mansion facing the River Ouse on the north-east side of Lindfield.

Standing in 5½ acres, including a wood and gazebo, Paxhill Park is built of ashlar stone — local Sussex sandstone — believed to have come from a nearby ruined nunnery.

Internally, there is a wealth of carved oak panelling, including Elizabethan figures depicting historical scenes. Two priests' holes have been blocked up during restoration work over the years.

Paxhill Park was owned by the Boord family until 1790, when the Crawfords took over until 1856, followed by Mr. J. W. Borsley.

Following owners were Herbert Noyes, then Northall Laurie, who restored the house and added the north wing in 1865, and William Sturdy, who added the south wing in 1877. Today Paxhill Park is run as a residential hotel and nursing home.

# Lindfield

Less than 100 years ago only vagrants lived in East Mascalls, a fine Elizabethan mansion in Lindfield. Then in the 1880's the derelict building was extensively renovated and in August of this year was sold privately for £170,000.

East Mascalls, a six-bedroom property dating from 1578, is built in the Cheshire style. The original East Mascalls occupied the same site before Edward IV's reign. It was bought in 1550 by Ursula Middleton, who later sold it to Sir William Newton, a member of an ancient Cheshire family related to Sir Isaac Newton.

William Newton gave it to his son Nicholas. He rebuilt East Mascalls in 1578, and it stayed in the Newton family until 1695. Restoration during the 1890's was by Mr. M. McNought.

Original features in the present day East Mascalls include oak joinery and beams, mullion windows and carved stone fireplaces. The house stands in about 2½ acres together with a five-acre paddock.

# Lindfield

The Thatched Cottage at Lindfield is an outstanding example of a pristine Wealden medieval house. The Thatched Cottage can trace its history back to the 14th century and the Chaloner family who built it. They came over in 1390 from Chalons in France where they were noted blanket makers.

In England they became wealthy farmers and dignatories in a purely local sphere — one of the family becoming the Vicar of Lindfield from 1569 to 1580.

Unfortunately, living at the cottage didn't help fertility too much because the male line became extinct around 1690.

The had meanwhile moved to a posher place next door which was handed down in later years to one John Studley, who married into the family, and later to the Pelhams, earls of Chichester.

The Thatched Cottage was the parish poor house and then again the manor house of Lindfield when the Chalomers were there.

Panelling is genuine Jacobean and the main construction of the house is oak framing with wattle and daub infilling. Large beams and uprights were cut by hand with saw and chisel from individual trees. All the curved timber was selected with its natural bend so as to fit in with building needs.

# Lindfield

The bread couldn't be fresher from Humphrey's Bakery in Lindfield High Street. But conversely the bakery from which it comes couldn't be older.

In fact some experts believe it is one of the three oldest buildings throughout the whole of Sussex and Surrey, a claim to fame if ever there was one!

The date of 1332 is the one given to the building. To live in it and its low ceilings, is a head-ducking experience for master baker David Wiles, his wife Jane and their children.

The family has been in the baking business for a respectable time. Mr. Wiles' father moved to Sussex from Ilford in 1942 to continue working this Lindfield bakery, established during the last century.

Today the cakes and bread are baked in a building built around 1900 and in a modern gas multi-oven. Before then the fuel used was coke which took over from the days of faggots.

# Lindfield

Cockhaise Mill Farm, Lindfield, was built around 1650 and parts of its probably go back even further. In 1958 a Bronze Age axe was found there — left by even earlier residents of the site.

The six-bedroom property is listed by the Government as part of the century's architectural heritage and the Cockhaise part of the label comes from a stream of that name which runs through the owner's land.

The mill which once went with the farm and which ground all the farm produce of yesteryear is still there. But today it is a neighbour's stylish house.

A family called Wildboar were once the local landowners, and a bridge over the stream is named after them to this day.

# Midhurst

The Wheatsheaf public house should satisfy drinkers with a taste for history.

The present building, overlooking Midhurst, on Rumbolds Hill, has a history stretching back nearly 400 years.

A plaque dates the two-storey building as being pre-Civil War. The plaque bears the initials ICW and the date 1621, when the building would have been a private house.

In the 18th century it was used for a time as a stable house and as a slaughterhouse. There are still remnants of stables in the rear yard.

The building has been a public house for over 200 years.

Originally it was just a beer house with no cider or spirits for sale, but since 1910 it has been owned by Sussex brewers King and Barnes.

The pub has flint and rubble walls and there have been few alterations to the outside since it was built.

# Midhurst

Suffice to say about the Spread Eagle Hotel at Midhurst that it is one of the oldest inns not only in Sussex, but in the country.

It dates back to the year 1430, which is the sort of antiquity for which absolutely no superlatives are needed.

Besides, there is nothing to add to how Hilaire Belloc described the Spread Eagle: "The oldest and most revered of all the prime inns of the world."

In its early days, the hostelry was known for its associations with the nearby mill and as a place where the great lords refreshed themselves during the chase.

Queen Elizabeth and her lords feasted and made merry there after hunting in the surrounding forests.

The spread eagle that forms the hotel's distinctive motif was the crest of the de Bohuns, mediaeval Lords of La Coudreye,

now Cowdray, who also owned the castle on St. Ann's Hill.

In the part of the Spread Eagle that dates back to 1430 there are fine timbered rooms, notably the Queen beam in the King's room, a favourite of Edward VII during his stays at Midhurst. In later years wig rooms were added to the bedrooms of the old building but otherwise they are to this day exactly as they were 500 years ago.

The "new" part of the hotel dates from 1650. The dining hall is graced by a fireplace as large and as beautiful as are the hams and Christmas puddings that hang from its beams.

There are Christmas puddings on the ceiling too, hung there at the request of travellers in the coaching days who, when spending a right royal and merrie Christmas, would reserve themselves a pudding and a place in the hotel for the next year, a charming tradition which is still honoured to this day.

# Newhaven

The year 1848 saw an unusual couple book into the Bridge Inn, at Newhaven, under the name of Mr and Mrs Smith.

Presumably they thought the name would be sufficiently inconspicuous to grant them the anonymity they sought. The pair were not runaway lovers, but King Louise Philippe of France and his queen — on the run from their rebellious subjects.

The Bridge Inn, in Bridge Street, has been in its key position in the town since 1623. It was at one time a brewery, called appropriately Clipper Ale, and doubtless vied with other local breweries like Tipper Ale for a share in the tastes of the townsfolk.

103

# Newick

Newick is a cosy village nestling in the Sussex countryside near Lewes.

Once it was a major resting place for religious travellers journeying between Canterbury and Winchester.

It was an ideal spot on the pilgrim trail, situated half-way between the two christian centres of worship.

The modern-day traveller might be tempted to dally a while in Newick, or even settle down there, if it meant living in such a desirable residence as Founthill Farm.

Once Simon and Matilda of Funte are said to have lived here in 1296, perhaps in an earlier house on the same spot.

Then it was said to be connected with the church and records show that the yearly rent was two shillings and sixpence.

In those days the stream on the northern boundary of the property was a navigable river and ran into the Ouse.

The present house was built about 1530 and the main part of it has been altered little since henry VIII's reign.

Inside is a world of history told in architecture. The oak staircase has the original Elizabethan newel post and there are authentic windows with filleted roll mullions, old fastenings and early diamond-pane glass.

The whole is bound together with timber framing, probably made from old ship timbers.

The wood has grown so hard over the centuries that it's virtually impossible to drive a nail more than a fraction of an inch into it.

It wasn't a problem that bothered early builders because in those days they never relied on nails or screws.

Sharp people they were in all ways — you can still see a place on the inglenook fireplace where the side was worn away by knife sharpening long ago.

# Northiam

Massive oak timbers from the Weald forest were used to build Great Dixter house more than 500 years ago.

The Manor of Dixter is first mentioned in 1220, but the oldest part of the present framed house, the Great Hall, dates from 1450. With an exceptionally large span, it is unique in having both hammer-beam roof trusses and also tiebeam and kingpost.

As a tumbledown farmhouse it was bought in 1910 by Nathaniel Lloyd and restored by the architect Sir Edwin Lutyens.

The contents include antique furniture of national importance and some very fine needlework, much of it worked by members of the Lloyd family who still occupy the house.

In the solar, the withdrawing room of the lord of the manor, the stone fireplace is original and the early fireback bears the personal emblems of the kings Henry VII and VIII.

The oriel windows have been restored. In the south one is a design on painted glass by Durer, dated 1518.

In the parlour it is possible to see an Elizabethan inscription on a beam above the piano. This refers to the tenant occupying the house when it was owned by Edward, third Lord Windsor and the Queen's representative at the court of Venice.

The house was first opened to the public 50 years ago.

# Patcham

All Saints Church at Patcham is of Norman origin, although that is only plainly visible from the inside.

It has a plain chancel arch, with two reredos recesses left and right, and a north doorway that has now been blocked in.

Externally, it is all 13th century; particularly typical of this is the thin west tower with small lancets as bell openings.

The north aisle is of late Victorian character, and seems to date from 1898.

Above the chancel arch is a painting, now re-drawn, of the Last Judgement, circa 1230. It show Christ enthroned, the rising of the dead and the weighing of the souls, also the Virgin and St John.

As for plate within the church, there is a cup with cover engraved 1568, and an engraved foreign pattern of 1666.

There is also a monument to Richard Shelley of 1594. It is in a fragmentary state with short, tapering pilasters, a coat of arms and grave diggers.

106

# Petworth

Petworth House is a late seventeenth century Baroque palace which seems to be all of one time. But the crowded irregularity of the east front reveals much earlier, and more complicated origins.

Until 1670 Petworth belonged to the powerful Percy Earls of Northumberland, who acquired it from Henry I.

All that can now be seen of their castellated house is the chapel, built about 1309 and incorporated into the body of the later house.

But beneath the Carved Room lies the undercroft of a mediaeval hall, and the long cellar under the rooms to the south of it was built by the ninth Earl, known as the Wizard because of his interest in scientific experiments, in 1625.

Had it not been for his suspected complicity in the Gunpowder Plot, for which he spent 16 years in the Tower, the Wizard Earl would probably have rebuilt Petworth.

In the event it was his great-granddaughter Lady Elizabeth Percy, and her husband Charles Seymour, Duke of Somerset, who set about the transformation of the house between 1688 and 1693, and who are largely responsible for its present appearance.

The third Earl, the patron of Turner, who often visited Petworth, added the sculpture gallery to the north front.

A final chapter in the architectural history of Petworth was Salvin's rebuilding of the southwest corner of the house, providing a more convenient entrance, in 1869-72.

# Petworth

Local dignitaries were surely upset when their 'local' opposite the Petworth town hall was demolished at the turn of the century.

The pub was the Half Moon, and must have been very conveniently sited for those who discovered Town Hall meetings left them with a dry throat.

But the site did not stay empty for long and in 1906 the London and County Bank opened a branch there.

The London County must have been prosperous as they had opened a branch in the town as early as 1846, moving in 1906 to the large Edwardian building in the square.

# Petworth

The parish church of St Mary dates back to Saxon times, when the village was known as Peteorde, and appears in the later Domesday Book of 1086.

The first recorded rector comes nearly 200 years later, and was Thomas de Falconberg who was instituted in 1238.

A later rector, William Blaker, in his will dated October 9, 1485, bequeathed "to the blessed Mary of Petworth one book, De Beata Maria Virginis" to remain perpetually chained in the chancel. Unfortunately the book did not survive the Reformation.

Most of the present building dates from the 13th and 14th centuries, but there were further additions in 1827 and 1903.

One of the most interesting aspects of the building is the tower, of which the lower part dates from 1350. There have been two steeples in the church's history.

The first, of wood and lead slanted dangerously to one side, inspired the old rhyme: "Proud Petworth, poor people. High church, crooked steeple."

This spire was removed in 1800, and was followed with a brick tower in 1827, which was designed by architect Charles Barry. At the same time the tower was raised 30ft. and became a Sussex landmark.

However, in 1947 this spire was found to be dangerous, and was demolished to be replaced by a parapet and low tiled roof.

# Pevensey

How about this for a town hall? There's many a modern ratepayer who would like to see the one in his own town — and his rates bill — cut down to a similar mini size.

But even 100 years ago the Court House at Pevensey was the smallest town hall in the country.

Today tourists visit a museum in the building and view a fascinating collection from Pevensey's past.

But once the death sentence used to be handed out in this tiny centre of justice.

The building incorporates restoration work carried out in the 18th century. Its general style and roof are Tudor, and some of the beams may belong to the original structure.

Directly below the Court House, with an entrance on the street, are two cells and a small yard where prisoners were allowed to exercise.

They are part of the museum now — but you never know when they might be needed again. For instance, in 1940, when Pevensey was steeling itself for a possible German invasion, the wooden bunks were lined with zinc so that the cells could be used as a mortuary.

Not for those occupants would there have been the chance to see an oak beam which is almost certainly the doorpost of an old cell, or the carved initials of offenders and a sorry statement by one luckless resident that he was forced to spend a month there.

Still on view are the weights and measures used in the borough to make sure penny-pinching tradesmen didn't diddle the local populace.

Smugglers weren't bothered with such measures, and there were plenty of them not so long ago. Their numbers were so great that they had pitched battles with the customs and revenue men, the last big one being recorded at the Pevensey Sluice in November, 1853.

Three smugglers were killed, five captured and many wounded.

# Poynings

Is there anything more restful than a Sussex Farm?

There probably is if you are a farm worker who has to turn out in all weathers, but if you are a harrassed town dweller, marooned in a sea of concrete, the sight of a place like Dyke Farm House is rustic ointment for fume-sore eyes.

The soil in which this soothing secret is rooted is that of Poynings, just tantilisingly over the hills inland from Brighton.

Here farm and village hug the lee of the South Downs as they have for centuries.

The farm is steeped in history. It is reputed to have originally been built as a manor house for Poynings and its architecture is a reminder of that original grand plan.

It is built around a small central courtyard and snuggles under a handmade clay tile roof behind leaded light windows and restful red bricks.

Once Dyke Farm House was owned by a family called Osbourne who at that time were also prosperous enough to have owned nearby Newtimber Place.

There are clues to its past in the actual walls themselves. On a stone on the south-side are inscribed the initials "W & M. O." and the date 1729.

History at Poynings, though doesn't stop there. This was a flourishing community more than one thousand years ago and is mentioned in the Domesday Book.

In the British Museum is proof of even greater antiquity. It is a document dated 962 and is a charter of the Saxon King Edgar who listed among hs possessions Puningas — the modern Poynings today.

The name itself has been interpreted as meaning "pond people".

The village church cements the image of quietness. It was built in 1369 but there was a wooden forerunner building for early Christians as far back as 800, and a stone church that filled the gap before the present and existing church was built.

# Pulborough

Envy the families who have lived in the Old House, Church Hill, Pulborough.

This mediaeval 15th century building has a grace that goes with its architecture, and its historic outline has sprung to life on the sketch pads of countless artists.

The property is a pristine example of a single hall house, as dwelt in happily by yeomen and farmers all those centuries ago.

In Sussex there are quite a number of such heritage gems but in other parts of the country they are thinner on the ground.

At the Old House the 17th century saw the grafting on of additions that made the accommodation more spacious.

But there is nothing that detracts from the original concept of the building, which, understandably enough, has attracted a Government grading as a house of historic interest.

Pulborough became a properous centre of Roman occupation, and two villas were linked to the famous Roman road called Stane Street.

The town was already adding to that early prosperity when the canal era came along.

The canal, which linked what was called the Arun Navigation

THE OLD HOUSE, PULBOROUGH.

to the Wey Navigation, climbed by a series of 14 locks from near Pulborough away up to the Surrey-Sussex border.

It doubtless came into its own in helping transport the well known Pulborough stone quarried in the area.

Here, too, there was in mediaevel times a priory chapel, the ruins of which can still be seen. The church is reached through a 14th century lych-gate and has a 15th century stone porch with a timber roof. The chancel dates all the way back to around 1220.

The fine tower and the nave and aisle were rebuilt around 1400. On the wall of the north aisle is a brass to remind us of Thomas Harlying, who died in 1423, and was rector at the church.

# Robertsbridge

Robertsbridge is part of the border land territories of Sussex where the character of the county begins to merge and form a unity with that of neighbouring Kent and its more immediately marshy areas.

This East Sussex village nestling in green countryside inland from Hastings takes its name from Robert De St. Martin, who founded the Robertsbridge Abbey in the 12th century.

To be more precise it was a Cistercian abbey of 1176 and the few remains of which are incorporated in the buildings of Abbey Farm south-east of Salehurst and reached by a track crossing the Rother.

A 13th century arch to be seen in the farmhouse is a remain of what was once probably the abbot's lodge. It soars over a vaulted crypt and to the east are the ruins of the abbey refectory.

Robertsbridge itself is set upon the slopes of a hill and has many timber fronted red-roofed cottages, some dating from the 16th and 17th centuries.

Time has taken some toll though. The fortnightly cattlemarket which could be traced right the way back to 1253 was transferred in 1954 to Battle and the Kent and East Sussex Light Railway, one of the last surviving railways and which ran to Headcorn, closed down at the same time.

But progress doesn't take care of every requirement and cricket bats are still made in Robertsbridge as they have been in the area since before the famous W.G. Grace wielded bats turned out by craftsmen here.

Indeed they are said to be the best bats available in England and they are made from the many willow trees grown in the area.

The tradition started about 1870 when a cricket enthusiast called L. J. Nicholls started shaping the odd bats for himself and his friends in the village.

# Rye

Durrant House, the Georgian building at the end of Market Street in Rye, looks an unlikely centre for military operations.

But in the 18th century it was purchased by Sir William Durrant, a close associate of Arthur Wellesley, who later became the Duke of Wellington.

And during the Napoleonic Wars the building became the centre for operations involving defence of the Channel ports.

It also served as a relay station for carrier pigeons bearing the news of a victory at Waterloo.

When it was built it was involved with the smuggling trade and John Wesley, who later stayed at the house during his evangelical tours, wrote: "Ryers do many things gladly, but they will not part with their accursed smuggling."

The involvement of the house with smuggling is shown by the many passageways and cellars which allowed easy means of escape.

# Rye

Fletcher's House, Rye was named after a famous Elizabethan playwright and poet who was born there while his father was a Minister in the town.

Fletcher collaborated with many famous playwrights of his age, including Shakespeare, Francis Beaumont, Massinger and Rowley. His The Faithful Shepherdess is regarded as one of the best English pastoral plays.

The house dates from the 15th century and is typical of the local design of that period. It is a long building with wings and a middle hall running east to west.

The sides of the building show ancient close studding to the upper storey, heavy floor beams and curved brackets.

The chimney stack has a moulded Tudor fireplace with carved spandrels and there are remains of the original 15th century framing on the king post roof.

# Rye

St. Peter's house in Rye was one of the many religious houses that suffered in the 16th century Reformation, during the reign of Henry VIII.

Previously this house, with its early English arch, mediaevel fireplace and sloping lean-to roof, was one large building enclosed by a stone wall.

But after the Tudor king's anti-religious sweep across England the building was divided up and its religious links quashed.

Then the building belonged to the plutocratical Lamb family and was part of the Lamb estate until it was sold about 150 years ago. It then became a clay pipe factory for a time.

# Rye

The House Opposite, in Mermaid Street, Rye, dates from the 16th century and was once a symbol of the town's prosperity. In common with many of the larger houses in Rye at the time, it was inhabited by merchants and shipowners.

Although the house was built in the 16th century, its foundations date from about the 14th century. The original building was destroyed in the great fire that swept the town at the end of the 1500s.

In the early 17th century, the chimney stacks at the east gable were installed, as was an extension.

The carved front doors, of Flemish origin, are hung upside down.

As the town's port silted up, the prosperity of Rye declined, and with it the fortunes of The House Opposite.

By the 18th century it became little more than a tenement, and in 1821 was divided into two properties, housing fisherman and artisans.

However, in 1924 the divides were taken down and the house restored to its former state.

# Rye

The Flushing Inn at Rye was the scene of a remarkable discovery at the turn of the century.

Early plasterwork was removed from behind panelling on the east wall of the old hall in 1901 to reveal a Tudor fresco.

The wall painting, which dates from the early 16th century, has now been renovated.

The fresco was originally executed in water colours with a thick skin of lime plaster forming the finishing coat.

It depicts scrolling foliage with numerous stylised animals and the Elephant and Castle symbol.

It is interrupted by three broad diagonal bands, each bearing the motto "soli deo honor et gloria", which roughly translates to "For the honour and glory of God alone."

The frieze also introduces Tudor roses, the coat-of-arms of Jane Seymour and the royal arms of England.

The artist is unknown, but the painting dates from about 1544 and originally formed a backcloth to the original dining hall.

The original Flushing Inn, in Market Street, Rye, is thought to date from between 1200 and 1250.

This building was destroyed by a fire after the French attack on the town in 1377. Today only the barrel-vaulted Norman stone cellar survives.

There are two theories of how the building acquired its name. The most likely is the street outside the inn was originally called The Butchery.

The name can still be faintly seen on the house at the corner of East Street and Market Street.

The old English name for a butcher was a fleshers, and it is thought the name became Fleshers Inn and was gradually corrupted to Flushing Inn.

# Sharpthorne

Smugglers once frequented the timbered rooms now used by guests at the Gravetye Manor Hotel, restaurant and country club at Sharpthorne, near East Grinstead.

Traces of the smugglers' lane that used to carry contraband to and from the house can still be seen inside the grounds.

And a stain on part of the original floor in the master bedroom is said to the blood of a village maid, murdered when she chanced upon the smugglers' secret hoard.

It was built in stone in 1598 by one Roger Infield for his bride Katherine Compton. Both were native to Sussex, and carved oak portraits of the couple can be seen above the fireplace in the master bedroom.

But perhaps Gravetye's most notable owner was William Robinson, one of the greatest gardeners, who bought the manor and its 1,000-acre estate in 1884.

It was his home until he died, well into his nineties, in 1935.

While at Gravetye he pioneered the creation of an English natural garden which became the pattern for many others throughout the country.

Even when confined to a wheelchair in later life, Robinson took an active interest in his garden, often going out to scatter bulbs and seeds from a bag on his lap.

It was William Robinson who enlarged and improved the manor, building the wing that now includes the dining room and extra bedrooms. He also added to the interior furnishings of the house, but took great care to preserve the Elizabethan style.

Labour shortages and economic difficulties hit the estate during and after World War Two, but since 1958 pains have been taken to establish Gravetye as a leader among premises offering country house hospitality.

It has been a successful venture, for Gravetye is now recognised by many leading gourmets and consumers organisations.

# Shipley

Today the Old Cottage in Shipley looks like a scene from a chocolate box. Who would have thought it was once a cow shed?

The original Sussex flint walls, some of which protected cattle from the elements as far back as 1620, are now rendered and pebbledashed.

"I know there's flint under there because every time I bang a nail in it breaks," said Mr Anthony Hawkins, the present owner.

He and his family suspect the Old Cottage was once part of the Langmead estate.

"This part of Sussex was really divided between three large families, the Langmead family was one of them" Mr Hawkins explained.

The cottage is in Shipley lane, about two miles from Bognor, and its thatched roof and porch and pink painted walls add to the picture-postcard look. It even has roses round the door.

Inside, the three-storey building has an inglenook fireplace, flagstones on the dining room floor and low ceiling beams.

# Shoreham

What's in a name? Where the Marlipins Museum, Shoreham, is concerned there's quite a lot, and it goes back a long way.

One meaning of the word pin is barrel. That's not too difficult, but what about the marl bit?

When the sophisticated Normans invaded England they found Saxons quaffing pints of mead and beer that turned their refined sense of taste. So they got down to organising frequent forays across the Channel taking their pins back to France to replenish their stocks and vaults.

But even in those days they couldn't go automatically through the customs green light, Marl is thought to have been a Saxon word meaning customs or excise.

And so Marlipins put together means literally, a tax on, or of,

the pins, with the museum probably being the place where they used to levy it.

It is probable also that the museum used to be a customs depot for a host of other goods coming into what was in those times as thriving a port as it is now.

The Marlipins is thought to have been built by the De Braoses, Lords of the Manor of Shoreham and Lords of the Barony of Bramber.

Deeds go back to 1347, by which time the family had died out and the Marlipins had already changed hands many times.

The contents, too, have reflected a nautical flavour since the building ceased its life as a carpenter's workshop, was bought by public subscription and opened as a museum by Sussex Archaeological Trust in 1928.

Ships models abound and a chief item of the collection is a replica of Seringapatam, made by Robert Butler, of Shoreham.

# Slaugham

Sussex is a county that has always been so well placed for London and which has contained so much charm in the past as now that hardly the smallest hamlet is without some intriguing historical link.

Take Slaugham for instance — or Slaffham as it is pronounced. It lies off the main A23 London to Brighton road near Handcross, a village of bright green grasses, colourful flowers and houses matured by the centuries.

The footsteps that once echoed down this village street played their part in protecting all we think of today as British.

They belonged to Admiral Lord Nelson, Britain's most famous sailor. He often used to visit Slaugham to escape the pressure of maritime life and to visit his sister Catherine, who was married to one George Matcham and who lived in the village at Ashfold Lodge.

It is today a place where a sailor would still gain a sense of

being ashore with a difference. In the churchyard of the parish church there stands an ancient yew tree about 25ft round.

And in the valley to the south-east are the ruins of Slaugham Place, the Jacobean mansion of the Converts, a family of some fame in the neighbourhood during the 16th and 17th centuries.

The church itself has a nave and chancel of Norman origin and a restored 13th century tower with a Sussex "cap". The whole building was extensively restored in the 19th century, but with discretion and tact.

The late Norman font is made of Sussex "marble" and has a symbolic feature unique in Sussex, a fish carved on one side. The word fish in Greek spells the initial letters of Jesus Christ. Wall paintings were also discovered here in 1859, but despite strenuous efforts crumbled in the atmosphere and could not be saved.

The greenery hereabouts is added to in summer by the delights of Slaugham park, occasionally open to the public.

Gerald Lip 1980

# Southover

Over 900 years ago a small group of Clunaic monks from France were given a small church at Southover, near Lewes, and almost immediately they started work on a new, larger stone church.

The French Clunaic order was at the height of its power and influence then and it was given the church by William de Warenne, who was trying to introduce the order to this country.

Just eight years later the monks completed their work and the Priory of St Pancreas stood on the flat land around Southover, ready to stretch its tentacles of religious reform across England.

William himself was buried in it, beside his wife who had died three years previously in 1085.

The late 11th century church is known only by excavations, but it seems in its final form it was nearly 450 feet long. The great

Abbey of Cluny in Burgundy, the centre of the order, was 650 feet long.

Like the Abbey, the Lewes priory has radiating chapels and two pairs of transepts — the part of a church at right angles to the nave.

The priory can be reached from Cockshut Road, next to the South Downs Tennis Club, but the original approach was from the north, where the great gate still remains.

It was built in the 13th century, of Sussex marble. The other entrance was re-erected at the western end of Priory Crescent.

Parts of the priory, dating back to 1140, are now in the British Museum and the Lewes Museum, and stones from the priory have been re-used in the gardens of Southover Grange.

# Southwick

The Schooner Inn, at Southwick, was originally built as a hotel in the 19th century, and still keeps its original fourfloor structure.

Whent it was a hotel it overlooked the towpath used by barges bringing in coal and timber.

A concrete bridge, called the Jubilee Bridge, spanned the canal, and was dug out by prisoners of Lewes jail in 1856. It used to connect the main road with the oyster beds on the river's opposite bank.

Today, however, oyster beds have given way to a power station.

# Stanmer

For more than 200 years Stanmer was the seat of and long established Sussex family, The Pelhams earls of Chichester since 1611.

But classically English though the house seems, it was actually designed by Nicholas Dubois, a Frenchman serving with the British Army.

Stanmer and its stables and outhouses were built between 1720 and 1727 at the height of the Palladian revival in building styles.

All the panache and expansiveness of the times is here. The grand oak staircase, for instance, was made by a Lewes craftsman and for only £35.

All told, it was a snip of a purchase when Brighton council acquired Stanmer House from the Chichester Trustees in 1947 for £250,000.

Even at that stage, though, there were bills to pick up. In residence before there had been the Army, who stayed in the house during World War Two, and who were more than robust in their occupancy,

Wet rot, too, had been another tenant and emergency restoration work required then was extensive and drastic.

But the house and stables (illustrated) came through it all. Once Stanmer was suggested as a site for the ancient buildings museum that eventually went down the coast to Singleton.

That opportunity was lost but the modest rural museum already run here by the Stanmer Preservation Society is just a pointer to potential still to be tapped.

125

# Steyning

At one stage the site of The Stone House in Steyning High Street must have been worth a mint — literally!

Until about 1100 the site held the Steyning Mint, which with the church was one of the oldest buildings in the village. The country then was dotted with numerous small mints.

What happened to Steyning Mint is not recorded, but the site was used later for The Stone House. A stone fireplace recently recovered dates from the 14th century, but records from the Abbey of Sian in 1476 could indicate the building was a good deal older.

In 1609, town records still show it as the Prison House, but this seems to have faded out of existence by Victorian times, as a record of houses there in that time gives it no name.

The original building had a flint and stone section, with a timber section in the upper part — a style commonly used during Elizabethan times. This was renovated with a brick facade in Georgian times.

# Steyning

There can be few better aims in education than "honesty and cleanness of life, kindly and decent speech, humility and courtesy and good manners."

Such were the ideals laid down by Chichester alderman William Holland in a deed dated June 16, 1614, when he decreed that a free school should be maintained at Steyning.

In fact what he founded was Steyning Grammar School, one of the oldest educational establishments in Sussex. Today it is one of the most prominent seats of learning in the county. The old buildings are still used in Church Street, in conjunction with a former secondary school at Shooting Hill on the town's outskirts.

But such a dream could only have been a wild fancy in the mind of William Holland back in 1614. Some say he could have endowed a school that had already been in existence as early as 1584.

And indeed there are grounds for belief that this may have been so. The old building in Church Street was originally Brotherhood Hall and was probably built by the Brotherhood of the Holy Trinity in the 15th century.

In those early days the school was limited to taking only 50

sons of gentlefolk and it established a reputation for achievement in Latin scholarship. The boys needed to excel — for they were allowed to talk only in Latin.

That wasn't the only stipulation which make today's regulations seem permissive. Pupils also had to pay a penny a quarter to buy the canes with which they were beaten.

It was the sort of schooling that either made or broke. One person it made was a John Pell, one of the most distinguished of Steyning Grammar School's pupils.

He was a maths genius and linguist, went to Trinity College, Cambridge, at 13 and was a BA in four years.

Cromwell sent him to Switzerland in 1654. This remarkable man became an Essex rector and was twice imprisoned for debts before he died in 1685.

# Steyning

An outwardly uninteresting slab of stone by a Steyning church could provide a vital clue to the village's origins.

The Steyning Stone, in the porch of St. Andrew's, served as the upper step in the east entrance for generations. But in 1938 it was disturbed during work on a new heating system.

It may have been a grave cover, but the unequal weathering suggests it could have been an upright stone similar to those found in Cornwall.

Evidence points to it being pre-Christian, and it may have later been "Christianised" by the addition of a small upright cross.

The first church of Steyning was built by St. Cuthman at the beginning of the ninth century, and later in 857 Ethelwulf, King of the West Saxons and Father of King Alfred, was buried there.

Tradition says the grave was outside the present church, in the corner now formed by the wall of the south aisle and the east side of the porch.

If that is correct, it would indicate this was the position of the original St. Cuthman's.

King Edward the Confessor, prior to 1047, gave the manor of Steyning with its church, to the Benedictine Abbey of Fecamp in Normandy. Thus, an early Norman cruciform stone collegiate church displaced the Saxon wooden one.

Harold then dispossessed Fecamp of the church and the manor, and held both until his death in 1066, when William the Conqueror renewed the gift to Fecamp and confirmed it by charter in 1085.

But the church's changes of ownership did not stop there, and in 1415 it passed, together with the manor to the Crown as a possession of "alien men of religion" and in 1461 was conferred by Edward IV upon the English Abbey of Sion in Middlesex.

# Steyning

A ten-bedroomed hotel in Steyning High Street once provided a different form of accommodation.

Springwells was formerly St. Cuthmans, and enjoyed the reputation of a boarding house/hotel under the ownership of the Misses Scott Maudlin.

The house itself was built in 1772 for the Georgian merchant who owned a business next door. The merchant is believed to have been either a tanner or a brewer.

The name was changed to Springwells about eight years ago, and boasts yew trees up to 200 years old. Planting several trees when the house was built was not an uncommon practice then.

129

# Stopham

Stopham House, built after the Norman Conquest of Britain in 1066, has links with one of the oldest families in the country. Brian Stopham, a knight at the Battle of Hastings, and his squire Adam Barttelot settled in the village after being given land grants of more than 4,000 acres.

It is said they could ride from Stopham village to Horsham without ever leaving their own land. The village itself lies one mile outside Pulborough, and was originally called Ford Place — after the ford over the River Arun in the parish.

The house came into the Barttelot family after Joan Stopham married John Barttelot.

Much of the house was rebuilt in 1787, again in 1842 by John Barttelot, and yet again in 1865. It boasts a Sweet Gum tree in its grounds, by the gate on the north side. The tree is more than 52 feet high, and measures more than 6ft in girth.

The most exceptional tree in the grounds however, is a plane tree more than 95 feet tall, with a girth of almost 23 feet. The Foresty Commission estimated it to be around 200 years old.

# Tarring

St. Andrew's Church at Tarring is an unusually large church for this part of Sussex.

It was restored in 1885, and large quantities of Italian mosaic were used.

Its design seems to represent the point in time where the early Gothic impulse spent itself in the county.

The best detail inside is a trefoil headed Piscina in the south aisle, and the tower and chancel are later, possibly representing Canterbury work, as the church has always come under the wing of the Archbishop.

The chancel has typical early perpendicular two-light windows, and a more elaborate and unusual east window.

As for the woodwork, there are two misericords in the chancel. They are late Gothic and the best pair are carved with a head. The rest have foliage carving.

# Upper Beeding

Upper Beeding is in a corner of Sussex that the retreating sea and coastline have left high and dry.

But then the Adur flows through there still and a sense of history at least hangs on, despite incursions made into the village life and fabric by the 20th century.

Beeding's history is tied up with its bigger next door neighbour, Bramber, which once boasted its influential castle. Bramber indeed spilt over into Beeding and one famous institution which ended up here was the Priory of Sele.

That came about when William de Braose, one of the Conqueror's knights, established a small college of clergy at the same time as work went on at the castle, and then topped it all by setting up a priory at Beeding.

It was linked up with the great abbey of St. Florent at Saumur on the Loire and hummed along quite nicely until the French connection was broken in 1396. It then lapsed to the Crown and was given to the Shoreham Carmelites until Henry came along with his Dissolution.

At that point its total value was put at a distinctly earthy £26 8s. 4d. The value was small because the priory was small — around 16 monks.

Great families at Beeding didn't end with Mr de Braose. After him came the Mowbrays. From them the parish passed by inheritance to the Howards and was sold by Thomas, Earl of Arundel, in 1642 to one Piers Edgcumbe, of Mt. Edgcumbe, Devon, which gentleman held it until 1760.

Mr Edgecumbe then sold out to Colville Bridger.

In the Domesday Book they'd all have had their estate referred to as Beddinges, an area which even then had for long been occupied by Saxons before Norman conquerors came on the scene.

Lower Beeding, of course, by an illogical feat of naming which seems a peculiar English quirck, is miles away to the north in St. Leonard's Forest.

# Warnham

The Tower at Warnham was built in 1890 by the chairman of the Prudential Insurance Company, Philip Harben. It formed part of the Warnham Estate, and was used to supply water to the buildings of the estate.

It became redundant when mains water was installed, and in 1963 the whole estate was broken up to become converted private homes.

The south east corner of the tower is a cupola which holds the spiral staircase to the top. There is also a clock with a large bronze bell which strikes the hours.

Although no longer serving its original function, the tower should survive for many years. It has three-foot thick stone walls at the base.

# Wartling Hill

School Farm House, at Wartling Hill, near Hailsham, dates back to around 1540, and derived its name from a nearby ancient school house. This building, however, was built 300 years before the school, which was demolished in 1962.

Recent modernisation revealed exposed beams, and enabled the present owners to make a chimney, built about the turn of the 17th century, a prominent feature.

The distinctive mushroom shaped yew tree near the house is though to be about 350 years old, and achieved its present shape in 1919, when the owners decided they had had enough of its branches brushing the tiles off the roof during storms.

# West Dean

A perfect house in a perfect setting is how Charleston Manor has been described by the architectural experts.

To date no one has disagreed, nor could they possibly on knowing this beautiful home at West Dean, hidden away in the Downs, near Cuckmere Valley, just along the coast from Seaford.

The house itself is steeped in history. West Dean is said to have been the centre of Southern England's fight against the marauding Danes.

Along with that goes the story of King Alfred, of burnt cakes fame, who apparently came here to build a palace and ended up, according to history, building a shipyard on a sealine which at that time conveniently came this far up the valley.

Certain parts of Charleston Manor date back to around 1080 when they were built for one of the Conqueror's stalwarts who decided to settle in the country he and his fellow Frenchmen had just invaded.

The date so soon after 1066 makes the manor one of the oldest occupied houses in Sussex, and the country come to that.

The original Norman section is most noted for its Romanesque windows.

Other parts of the property have been traced back to 1200. The manor, of course, incorporates the later architectural styles that have represented the additions to it so that today it is a collection of the best of Norman, Tudor and Georgian.

The great Tithe Barn at Charleston is another slice of manor history and the venue for most of the events at the Charleston Festival.

# West Grinstead

Two legends are credited for the name of Bowshots house near West Grinstead.

The first is that in Henry V's reign two men had a wager over two greyhounds. Whoever won was to have the land which reached a bowshot's length from the house.

The other legend says the house was once a favourite meeting place for archers, who described it as being situated "a bowshot from the main road."

Bowshots is a pre-Tudor house of wattle, daub and oak, and later of brick and oak. It has a hipped roof, and original beams and floors are still visible.

At one time it was divided into two cottages and then later rejoined. The front entrance has a heavy oak studded floor.

Bowshots was once a farm, part of the vast Goring estates, and the Wiston archives reveal the following information: "26 August 1791 — attested copy of the sale for £134 from Chas. Goring to Thomas Billingshurst, of West Grinstead, brickmaker, and Thomas Evershed, of Billingshurst, a tanner."

Later the archives note: "Memorandum of agreement between Mary Goring, as guardian of Chas. Goring, with the tenant of Bowshots, John Robinson, 'half manure rights,' quantity 45 cartloads, each containing 30 bushels, March 1833."

Earlier this century Bowshots was owned by Sir Ralph Harwood who was treasurer to the Royal Family, particularly to Queen Mary.

# West Tarring

Five and six year olds now sing their hymns and say their prayers in a hall that was once the domain of archbishops.

The Old Palace at West Tarring is used for assembly by the pupils of the Thomas A'Becket School.

The youngsters have their lessons in the cluster of buildings which includes the Old Palace in Glebe Road.

Tradition associates the building in particular with Thomas A'Becket, although it is unlikely that he had much spare time to visit it while he was archbishop.

West Tarring was given to Christchurch, Canterbury, by King Athelstan, who died in AD 941.

From early times it is likely that the Old Palace was a stop-over point for archbishops of Canterbury where they could stay when journeying through Sussex.

Records say it is fairly certain that a manor house of some kind existed on the site in Becket's time.

Becket had early associations with Sussex. As a youth he is said to have spent a lot of time at Pevensey Castle and was later Dean of Hastings.

Eventually the Old Palace passed into Royal hands. Then at the end of the 15th or beginning of the 16th century it became the rectory, and manorial courts were held there.

In the early years of the 19th century it was partly occupied by cottagers. Then it became a Church of England school but had to be closed around the turn of the century because of epidermics.

But it soon opened again — this time as a State school. Until 1964 it housed the only school in West Tarring.

But then the new building in Bellview Road was opened. The old buildings still belong to the church and are let out for use by the school and other bodies.

# West Hoathly

Priest House is an early 15th century clergy house of timber construction with wattle and daub filling, and topped by a splendid Horsham slab roof. The house stands on a stone and timber base.

In its early days the property was probably just a hall with open timber roof and a hearth in the floor centre. The house was originally owned by the great Cluniac Priory of St. Pancras at Lewes.

They obtained permission from the Pope in 1391 to appropriate the "rectory" — the great tithes — of West Hoathly, appointing a vicar to serve the church and other parishes.

It is probably at this time that the small manor of the rectory of West Hoathly came into being and Priest House was built for its headquarters.

More fascinating still, West Hoathly men took an active part in the rising of Jack Cade in 1450 and Priest House may well have been the scene of discussions on how to recruit for the uprising. Lewes monks and their prior were openly on the side of the rebels.

In 1524 the Priest House was let by the priory to a tenant farmer; in 1538 it was among property seized from Lewes Priory by Henry VIII; soon afterwards it was given to the king's secretary, Thomas Cromwell; and after his execution in 1540 it landed up in the ownership of Anne of Cleves.

Round about 1560 Priest House was bought from Queen Elizabeth, into whose possession it had passed. Then the fine Tudor chimney and a floor dividing the hall into two storeys were added.

In 1965 it was sold to pay off debts and was bought by a Mrs. Hooper from faraway Barbados. By now it was becoming a trifle dilapidated.

But shortly after the property was saved for posterity by a Mr. John King.

# West Hoathly

The powerful Infield family of West Hoathly made their fortune from Wealden iron.

Forests surrounding the area were rich in the ore and the Infield coffers grew. The iron was sold to make armaments for the English army and navy.

Some of the Infield iron ore wealth was used to build West Hoathly manor house in 1627.

Then the Jacobean-style manor was called the Great House. The lord of the manor, a man named Brown, lived at the priest's house.

In 1670, there was a marriage between an Infield daughter and a Brown son. The couple moved into the Great House which, in time, became the Manor House.

For almost 200 years the house was let to a series of tenant farmers. In 1906, it was bought by John Godwin King.

The outer shell was intact but internally the manor house was in a poor condition. Mr King renovated the building and added extra rooms as servants' quarters.

During the last war the manor was requisitioned by the army as a headquarters and was visited by George VI.

Mr King's grandson, historical biography author Mr Jasper Ridley, now owns the eight-bedroom manor which he lets out.

Much of the internal panelling, beams, staircase, and fireplaces from the original 17th century building have survived.

# Wilmington

The origins of the famous Sussex landmark The Long man of Wilmington remain a baffling mystery to historians.

It is cut into the turf on the north side of the Downs, near Wilmington Priory, and in 1873 was outlined in yellow bricks.

The most prominent theory on its origin is that it dates from the Bronze Age and is about the same age as the Cerne Abbas Giant in Dorset. The present outline of The Long Man or the Wilmington Giant was laid out in 1969.

The lengths of the east and west staves are 230ft. 8in. and 235ft. 8in. respectively. The distance between the staves measures just over half their mean length.

Because of the slope of the hillside, anyone standing close by sees the figure as broad and sturdy, with the breadth exceeding the height.

# Wilmington

Wilmington Priory was formerly one of the possessions of the Benedictine Abbey of Grestain in Normandy.

It was given to the Norman abbey by the founder's son, Robert de Mortain, who came over with William the Conqueror in 1066.

Due to its convenient position by the sea, Wilmington Priory soon became the headquarters for the abbot of Grestain's representative in England.

There were probably two monks representing the abbey and they used Wilmington as a base to visit the abbot's other properties.

During the religious wars with France in the 13th and 14th centuries England took possession of all foreign priories, including Wilmington.

After this the priory and its lands was let to the highest bidder. It appears the priory building declined during this period because the tenants were more interested in getting money from using the land.

In 1565 Wilmington passed to Sir Richard Sackville and was later let to Thomas Culpepper, who, with his widow and nephew, is buried in the church.

In about 1700 the Wilmington estates passed to Spencer Compton, afterwards Duke of Wilmington, and then by marriage to the Cavendish family.

From this time successive farmers lived in the priory building until 1925, when the building was conveyed to the Sussex Archaeological Trust.

From its history the priory gives the impression of being more a manor than the usual monastery.

Its distinguishing feature is that it connected directly to the church via the south aisle.

The 12th century chancel was undoubtedly the monk's quire, while the nave was used for parochial worship.

# Winchelsea

This is the Strand Gate, Winchelsea. Thousands of artists have painted it, countless thousands of cars have passed through it on the road from Rye. And actress Dame Ellen Terry once used to live in the cottage next to it before she moved to Kent in 1900.

Small wonder, then, that Strand Gate has become one of the most famous portals in Southern England.

Like "New" Winchelsea, it dates back to Edward I. He created this village from virgin land in 1292, probably to control the then-important estuary of the River Brede.

Strand Gate is one of three surviving gate-houses in the wall erected around his new community by King Edward.

It has two narrow archways and four round towers that were in all probability at one time much higher.

From its commanding position throughout the centuries men have watched the tides of history sweep in all their turbulence over this now peaceful village.

"Old" Winchelsea had been a port of some note even in 1066.

It was added to the Cinque Ports and was confirmed as part of Hastings in 1191.

But it developed more quickly than either Rye or Hastings to become the most important sea town in Sussex of the time. The tide of events turned against the old town in the mid-13th century when the sea began literally to eat its way into the coast.

In 1266 it took the side of Simon de Montfort against Henry III and was besieged and taken by Prince Edward.

And finally the great storm of 1287 changed the course of the Rother, laid new foundations of prosperity for Rye and finally destroyed Old Winchelsea.

The new settlement was laid out in 800 plots for which an annual rent was paid directly to the Crown. Eventually it began to flourish again and became an outlet for the Sussex wool trade.

But attackers from across the sea were never far away. Winchelsea was attacked by the French repeatedly during the 14th and 15th centuries and was sacked by them in 1380.

Nature then took a hand when its harbour began to silt up. Elizabeth I visited here in 1573 but the village never quite regained its commercial or maritime importance again.

# Wisborough Green

Sparr Farm at Wisborough Green was built in 1394, by John le Sparre, and is thought to have been used as a manorial courthouse.

In the times of the manorial system, the lord of the manor would hold regular court sessions, and the locals would be pressed into jury service.

The word Sparr meant in early English, 'clearing in the woods', so it appears the house was one of the first in the village.

It is also possible that "clearing" referred to the animal pound that was sometimes built near the court house.

Many manorial court cases referred to villains' (peasants) animals that had wandered from the common grazing land on to the Lord of the Manor's property.

The creatures would be held in the pound until the result of the ensuing court case was decided.

In later years the house was owned by Jean Carre, the master of the local glassworks. He is thought to have lived here during the 16th century, and one of the nearby fields is named glass house field, the site of the glass works.

The property was restored in the Thirties and has an unusual half-tiled Horsham stone roof. It is now used as a guesthouse, attracting visitors from as far away as America.

# Worthing

Steyne Gardens Church in Worthing is a tribute to the growth of Methodism in the town. It was opened on June 20, 1900, at a cost of £6,200 to cater for "increasing numbers."

Methodism first began in Worthing in 1824. Two years later the first chapel was built in Marine Place. By 1840 a further chapel was needed and the premises in Bedford Row were built.

The numbers continued to grow, to the point when, in 1900, the Steyne Gardens Church was built in Brighton Road.